Charles Swain

Art and Fashion

With other Sketches, Songs and Poems

Charles Swain

Art and Fashion
With other Sketches, Songs and Poems

ISBN/EAN: 9783744775809

Printed in Europe, USA, Canada, Australia, Japan

Cover: Foto ©Thomas Meinert / pixelio.de

More available books at **www.hansebooks.com**

ART AND FASHION:

WITH OTHER

Sketches, Songs, and Poems.

BY

CHARLES SWAIN,

AUTHOR OF "THE MIND," "ENGLISH MELODIES," ETC.

LONDON:
VIRTUE BROTHERS & CO., 1, AMEN CORNER,
PATERNOSTER ROW
1863.

SHALL Indolence enchant the poet's lyre,
Yet Industry awake no kindred song?
Spirit of Commerce, hear! thy son inspire:—
Show him thy seas where masts, like forests, throng;
Thy sails each breeze of heaven impels along,
An universal presence o'er the tide!
Tell him where'er mankind hath heard thy tongue,
Intelligence hath march'd with rapid stride,
And mental freedom sprung rejoicing by thy side!

TO

JOHN PENDER, ESQ., M.P.,

AS A

LIBERAL PATRON OF ART,

AND AS ONE

ILLUSTRATING THE CHARACTER

OF A

BRITISH MERCHANT,

This Volume,

WITH EVERY SENTIMENT OF REGARD

AND ESTEEM,

IS GRATEFULLY DEDICATED.

CONTENTS.

ART AND FASHION
REYNOLDS
GAINSBOROUGH
HAYDON
LEONARDO DA VINCI
GIULIO ROMANO

SONGS AND POEMS.

THE CHAPEL-BELL
ENDURANCE
YEARS TO COME
"NIGHT" AND "MORNING"
THE BEST ESTATE
IN MEMORIAM.—HENRY MARSDEN
THE WANDERER
A DAILY SCENE
THE VICAR'S BLIND DAUGHTER
CRADLE SONG
THE WOODLAND WAY

CONTENTS.

	PAGE
NOT MY OWN	117
FREAKS OF FATE	118
WATCHING AND WAITING	120
PAN'S DEW-DROP	122
THE MEADOW GATE	125
BE SURE YOU CALL	127
FALSE AS WATER	129
LOVERS' WALKS	131
THE DEVOTED	133
PLAIN FACES	135
NEVERMORE	136
DID YOU KNOW HER?	138
NEVER FOUND	140
SMALL GIFTS	142
LYRIC	143
ROUND THE CORNER	145
A WORD OF THINE	147
THE BRITISH PRESS	149
BIRTHDAY LYRIC	154
CHRIST BLESSING LITTLE CHILDREN	157
IMPLORA PACEM	160
LINES ON THE DEATH OF MISS FLEMING	162
HELP EACH OTHER	164
A DAY AGO	166
GOOD ADVICE	168
THE MERRY HEART	170
THE MAGIC GLASS	172
PAST AND PRESENT	174
THE FORTRESS	175

CONTENTS.

LINES ON THE DEATH OF SIR JOHN POTTER, M.P.
OLD FRIENDS AND OLD TIMES
WHAT IS THAT WE TAKE FROM EARTH?
TO THE YOUNG
A HEART FOR EVERY ONE
MAIDENHOOD
THANK GOD FOR ALL
THE CROSS OF CHRIST
THE OLD EVENINGS
THE CHARITIES OF LIFE
LITTLE REQUIRED
EVERYBODY'S GIPSY
WHAT'S YOUR OPINION?
THE WHEREWITHAL
PASSING AWAY
DEAD, YET UNDIVIDED
THE HOPES GONE BY
FLOWERS
SYMPATHY
MORN
THE HIDDEN DELL
THE SOUL
AN EARLY VISITOR
BLAME ME NOT
THE DEAD SWAN
THE LOST ONE FOUND
TORQUATO TASSO
ADAM
WAITING FOR THE COUNTESS

CONTENTS.

	PAGE
YOUTH AND AGE	251
RIVA DI SAN MARCO	253
THE ANGEL'S CALL	257
ALL THINGS FOR GOOD	259
THE FLOWER SPIRIT	261
THE SHIP OF HEAVEN	263
THE EVE OF ST. JOHN	267
NOT TO-NIGHT	271
PRIZES AND BLANKS	273
THE TEMPLE	275
THE HEART	276
THE CAPTIVE	278
EARTHLY BEAUTY	281
DESPONDENCY	283
FAITHFUL AND FAITHLESS	284
ANGELS	286
LOVE THEE?	287
MY LIFE WAS LIKE A FOUNTAIN	289
THE FALSE ONE	291
BALLAD	293
WILL HE COME?	295
THE CAMP IS UP!	296
LITTLE THINGS	298
SOIL OF ENGLAND	300
MARY	302
THINKING OF OTHER DAYS	304
LET NOBODY KNOW	306
WAIT TILL I PUT ON MY BONNET	308
THE GARDEN STREAM	310

CONTENTS.

	PAGE
THE HAND OF A FRIEND	311
WIFE OF THE PIRATE	312
THE DAWN	315
VOYAGE OF LIFE	317
THE LONELY HOME	319
WHICH HOME?	322
THE WORLDLY VOICE	324
NE'ER WILL I FORSAKE THEE, MOTHER!	326
A LAMENT	327
FIRST EMOTIONS	328
THE DOOMED CITY	329
LOVE UNTOLD	332
THE SNOW SHIP	333
THUS NATURE SPEAKS	335
HYMN TO THE CROSS	336
HERMIONE	341
GOD HELP THE ORPHAN	348
LINES ON THE DEATH OF HENRY DRINKWATER BIRCH	351
FINIS	352

ART AND FASHION.

ART AND FASHION.

Ferdinand, *a young Artist.*
Augusta, *his Cousin.*

Scene—*An Artist's Studio; busts, casts, draperies, fishing-rods, &c., &c., lying about.*

ferdinand *at his easel, singing.*

Love said to Apollo one day,
   Can't you paint me a likeness of Venus?
If not by yourself, I dare say
   We might manage to sketch her between us.
But Venus declared, when she saw
   The image o'er which they'd been teasing,
That a child might be able to draw
   A portrait more perfect and pleasing.

Ah me! not e'en the gods can Beauty please!
Who'd be a portrait painter? Better slave

At any trade . . . . . better . . . . . (*singing*)

"A child might be able to draw."

Could I but realise Imagination,
Give permanence to Fancy, it were well;
But brighter visions visit me in dreams
Than, waking, I can execute. Sleep, sweet sleep!
Thou seem'st the soul of Art; king of a world
In which all others but resolve themselves!
Thine is the key to the impossible,
The wonderful, the magical—(*a knock at the door*).

     · Come in!
   If sprite or fay,
  Make good thy way,
And what thou mean'st by coming, say!

Enter AUGUSTA, *dressed in the extreme of fashion.*

FERDINAND.

Ah! Cousin mine, a thousand, thousand welcomes!
My eager hand hath scarce thy portrait left.
Methinks the head doth credit to my skill;
It fills the room with life—effuses light;
When cover'd, all seems dark. How lik'st thou it?

AUGUSTA.

Why, yes: 'tis like, no doubt, ... but . . . .

FERDINAND.

But!—
"A child might be able to "—
Your pardon, coz;
I deem that portrait, sketchy though it seem,
As near the sweet perfection of thy face
As hand can limn; the likeness free and true.
But for the dress—I am a bungler there;
The trimming is fantastic, and the rest
Needeth some toning down.

AUGUSTA.

Oh, that is easy!

FERDINAND.

You think 'tis easy, then, to catch " a likeness,"
Copy a nose, a mouth, a chin! You're right.
But copying nature is not all that's needed;
Something behind, unfeatured and unnamed—
The dewy light that rims the morning cloud
And lends a life to what was dull and cold—
Such is the light the Artist hath to find,
Else may the portrait show but spiritless.

AUGUSTA.

Certes, a face is like a lamp unlit

Without the mind; it is the living mind
That shapes expression.

####### FERDINAND.

I know an Artist—
Ay, a great one too, his name still famous--
Who to each sitter took the callipers,
And measured, inch by inch, each feature's place,
Position, and proportion; after that—

####### AUGUSTA.

He took his canvas (*smiling*).

####### FERDINAND.

No such thing, my coz!
He made a drawing, finish'd and exact,
So bold, so vigorous in execution,
The after painting scarce could rival it;
In fact, the drawing beat the canvas oft.
There was a subtle sentiment he lost
In the translation: still he persevered,
Slowly, yet all determined to excel.
No toil thought he too much; knowing right well
Mere feature's truth is not true portraiture.

####### AUGUSTA.

You paint not thus?

FERDINAND.

    No : I rub in at once;
Yet question if 'tis quicker in the end.
I alter and re-alter; at my whim
Touch and re-touch. That mouth, which seems so slight,
Cost me some hours; I've had it in and out
Full twenty times: at length I took a book,
When, all at once, I saw the matter clear;
A few light touches, and the lips had life;
The portrait spoke: that is—

AUGUSTA.

     It should have done !
But this would seem a thing of chance, not Art;
One happy moment, worth ten studious hours !

FERDINAND.

Right—and yet wrong; the myst'ry deeper lies.
The thing to catch is not the outward shape;
Mere form a common copyist may reach;
But inward feeling, sentiment, emotion—
The mind that in its subtle currency
Illuminates each lineament, and gives
At different moments different effects—
'Tis this the Artist tries. . . . . .

ART AND FASHION.

AUGUSTA.

    No doubt, no doubt;
One cannot reach the soul with compasses,
Nor take its depth, nor breadth, nor altitude.

FERDINAND.

You've seen my Hamlet? Well, it cost some thought;
The critics gave me credit for the "*Ghost.*"
A presence, vague and supernatural—
A shade majestic, worthy of the realm
It left for earth : for that they proffer'd praise
Which cost the slightest trouble. 'Twas the mien,
The mind of Hamlet task'd my utmost power;
Again the mouth proved difficult to hit,
And for a week it ran a daily change.
At last, *one touch :* lo! 'twas the right effect;
A nervous, sensitive, expressive mouth.
The critics lent no echo to my Hope
That therein would my better fame be found,
But praised the Ghost!—
    The Ghost!—well, Fame's a ghost,
And Hope, too oft, a false Astrologer.
Talking of that—of Hope—you like not then
The portrait?

AUGUSTA.

If tongue may freely breathe it,
I much the portrait of our Aunt prefer.

FERDINAND.

Our Aunt dress'd simpler. What can mortal do
With all this heap of frill and frippery?
Art hates gay trimmings: they distract the eye.
What lovelier to a lovely countenance
Than plain attire—simplicity of garb?
I tell thee, Fashion, like a climbing weed,
Destroys the very thing it feeds upon!
Saw'st thou e'er graft upon a nobler stock,
On alder, oak, laburnum, sycamore?
The active root develops its own life
In vigorous shoots from out the parent stem
But these, at once, the gardener destroys:
The nature of the tree is sacrificed
For the more gaudy, showy, flaunting graft!
'Tis thus with you the graft of Fashion shows
Upon a nobler nature.

AUGUSTA.

Indeed! I . . .

FERDINAND.

Nay, stay and hear the rest. As feeds that graft
On qualities superior to its own,
Shoots, born to rise and soar, and drink the air
That circles nearer heaven, so Fashion preys,
So feeds, on Nature's purer elements.
Nature and she are foes. She, Fashion, stands
Cold, artificial, ever in extremes;
She dwells within the world without a heart;
Convention is her god, all vulgar else,
And than be vulgar better not be born.

AUGUSTA.

I'll hear no more.

FERDINAND.

Vulgar! what means the word?
Nothing's so vulgar as the light of day,
Which sits in hovels and lies down with rags;
Nothing's so vulgar as the breath of life,
Which e'en a rat holds equal with one's self;
Nothing—

AUGUSTA (*passionately*).

I thought you'd end in nothing!—
Now hear *me*. Fashion—grant me patience!
'Tis profanation thus to libel her.

ART AND FASHION.   11

She's the world's mirror : people see themselves
As she reflects them, or they see not life ;
They breathe but in the presence of her power.
Beauty lends homage due, which *she* repays
By making Beauty still more beautiful,
Form more attractive, feature more divine ;
A grace inspired by her supremacy,
And reach'd but by her vot'ries.   [*Walks about.*
     Fashion ! yes :
A thousand servants wait upon her steps :
All hands are busy for her.   Ships at sea,
Freighted with charms, obey her welcome summons.
She keeps the " World " in busy agitation ;
Shore, quay, and bustling wharf, warehouse and shop,
Teem with her queenly orders.   She keeps state,
And every stone grows hot with rolling wheels ;
She languishes, and every trade falls dull.
Fashion, indeed ! you teach where you've to learn.
I tell thee, Painter, let but Fashion take
Thy genius by the hand—let her but speak—
And she will turn thy palette into gold,
Transmute thy colours into costly gems ;
Patrons, in throngs, shall lounge about thy doors,
And Peers outbid each other for the next
Great effort of that hand which Fashion crowns
With her supreme distinction.   Fashion !

FERDINAND.

What humour's this? lo, what a heat you're in!—
Eye, cheek, and lip, glowing with lovely fire;—
A moment sit and let me paint you thus,
                [*Augusta walks about.*
Each ringlet trembling with strange brilliancy;
Passion becomes you; what a look was there!

AUGUSTA.

Ferdinand! . . . .

FERDINAND.

Well, Cousin!

AUGUSTA.

      Speak where you will,
But never more to me; never . . . .

FERDINAND.

          For what?
Well may sincerity be rare on earth.
The face belie the feeling, tongue shun truth—
                [*A pause.*
Nay, if thus hurt then am I grieved indeed.
Augusta!

AUGUSTA.

     Taunts, taunts, taunts, nothing but taunts!
For ever rating me, and scouting Fashion.

FERDINAND.

Because I love—nay, patience—Nature best!—
And yet not Nature more than I loved you,
Ere Fashion won you! Loved you! yes, *love still*—
Though Fashion seek to cast my quiet life
Too far apart from its divinity!
I worship—but the shrine finds other fires,
And burns to other gods!—

AUGUSTA.

To be so school'd!

FERDINAND.

You'll give your hand?

AUGUSTA.

To be so lectured!
Ever we meet to rail, even now you rail—
You that should kinder be than any one.

FERDINAND.

Well, let me own there's *truth* in what you spoke
Of Fashion and her power; yet I prefer
To satin robes, and lace, rich gems and flowers,
Some Indian village, by some shore remote—
Some Mohawk, with his arrow and his bow,
Full of that fire immortal Nature lit

When she created Man, whose bounding limb,
Instinct with power—alive with energy—
Ennobled every motion with a grace,
To which—now pardon me—to which, dear coz,
Fashion is manner'd, artificial, cold;
An image, not a being—sign, not fact:
A symbol, not a soul! But I have done—
Now on my *last* work give me your decree.

  [*Brings forward a picture, showing village home,
   with garden, field, and lane, and distant spire.*]

   AUGUSTA (*after a pause*).
Our cottage-home—our dear old cottage-home—
The spot a mother's early love made holy!
The very lane my school-led footsteps stray'd,
Rough with tall fern, and early fox-glove bells,—
The mossy spring round which the village maids
Would tell their merry secrets; whisper tales
Of moonlight meetings,—stories out of school,—
Things little birds had told them—happy days!
That gather'd pleasure from the simplest source.
Sweet days, so fresh with memory's morning dew,
What have ye left like that ye took?

        Oh Home!
We never prize thy worth till thou art lost,
And then—how dear, how exquisitely dear!—

FERDINAND.

All things are dear when sorrow shows their worth ;
Let but a moment be the scanty space
Between farewell and absence from the loved,
Unknowing the far period of return ;
And every simple, trivial, common thing
Becomes array'd with triple interest.

AUGUSTA.

The gate, the tree, the little garden-chair,
The shady corner where the bird-cage hung ;
A leaf—a flower—how do they spring to worth
When the heart pains to lose them? Would that all
Could learn to prize *before* compell'd to lose !
How many would be rich that think they're poor?
How many happy that are discontent?
How many pining, fretful natures *blush*
To show themselves before true sorrow's face ?—
Oh home ! oh mother !—oh too early lost !
I seek ye, but a grave is all I find !

FERDINAND (*aside*).

Nature speaks now.

AUGUSTA.

That mother, Fred, you loved her dearly *once*.

FERDINAND.

May memory scorn me when I love her not:
All that I am is owing to her worth;
An orphan 'neath her care,—her brother's child!
She must have loved that brother passing well,
For oft I've known her gaze on me with tears,
And wet my cheek with kisses! When she *died*—
No, no! not died, such goodness never dies!—
But when God's angels bore that saint to heaven,
A letter on her pillow lay, address'd
" To her young painter," whom she pray'd might win
A name among Earth's gifted. On one page
(I've read it oft, dear cousin, oft 'mid thoughts
That blinded me with tears)—on one page
She gave her daughter to a heart she knew
Honestly loved her with a manly truth,
Deep, firm, and lasting as the pulse within,—
But you—you have discarded the poor painter.

AUGUSTA.

You would not have a hand without a heart?
Such legacy could not enrich the heir!

FERDINAND.

Enforced affection? What? Against thy will—
Receive a cold, reluctant, backward heart?

Never! Oh God, that letter!
    [*He seizes the letter, and attempts to destroy it.*
And yet, thy mother's last, last written lines,
That loving, tender—no, I cannot tear,
But I can yield it! Never more my cheek
Shall sweetly slumber o'er the hope *it* gave;
My pillow never more its seal shall press
Whilst far in dreams I clomb the steep of fame,
And offer'd name and fortune at thy feet:
Dreams—oh delusions!—dreams that break the heart!
One kiss, dear seal—old friends should kiss at parting.
Now . . . . quickly . . . . take it!

           AUGUSTA.

Alone?

           FERDINAND.

    How mean you?

           AUGUSTA.

Not take the honest hand which holds the letter?

           FERDINAND.

Be merciful—be candid—be sincere:
Mistake not sudden sympathy for love.
You hesitate, ... you do not take the letter.

AUGUSTA.

Not hesitate—if, if you think my life
Can make your own more happy; if my love
Can make existence brighter in your sight;
Can—can reward you for the love I know
You cherish for your giddy, graceless cousin,
Then . . . .

FERDINAND.

Then . . . .
Oh, sainted shade—inheritor of heaven—
Who wert my friend, my *one* true friend on earth,
My parent when I needed parent most,
Look down, sweet saint, and bless thy grateful children!

AUGUSTA (*after a pause*).

This picture—

FERDINAND.

Well?

AUGUSTA.

It never must be sold.

FERDINAND (*struggling to recover his usual tone and feeling*).

So; every artist his own purchaser.
'Twere pleasant could it last; but much I fear
Such system scarcely may become the " Fashion !"

AUGUSTA.

Fashion? again, again!

FERDINAND.

An artist's wife . . . .

AUGUSTA.

Seeketh no fleeting aid of ornament.
But how we talk!—you were defeated, Sir:
The victor, not the vanquish'd, proffers terms!

[Exeunt.

REYNOLDS.

Scene—*Dining-room in* Sir Joshua's *house, Leicester Square.*

Enter Reynolds *and* Goldsmith.

REYNOLDS.

But when was this?

GOLDSMITH.

Less than an hour ago.

REYNOLDS.

Garrick and Johnson quarrelling on Art,
And questioning " the Beautiful "—what then?

GOLDSMITH.

Johnson declared all Beauty was a dream—
A fiction merely; something people saw
But through their fancy; and as Fancy chose
The jade misled her idle votaries.

REYNOLDS.

Pleasant, indeed! How came the subject on?
Johnson lacks faith in painting: he avers
That pictures are but toys—things to please babes.

GOLDSMITH.

The Doctor's weak of sight, and roughly speaks.

REYNOLDS.

But strong of mind; and, 'faith, he argues well.
Proceed with their discourse—how prosper'd it?

GOLDSMITH.

" Beauty," quoth Garrick, " is not definite;
There are no *general* principles for Beauty.
The features which delight us in one face
May suddenly displease us in the next.
Beauty is not a thing for square or rule."
" Sir, I deny it," Johnson, growling, broke;
" There *is* a settled principle of Form,
Which, injured, you beget deformity.
Rule?—Nature, Sir, submits herself to rule!
One thing is needed you to judge aright—
Discrimination."
                    " I cannot comprehend,"
Said David, stiffly, ...

"Of course you cannot—
People, too oft, are slow of comprehension.
Beauty, good lack! what knowest thou of it,
Except in paint and foil? Beauty, with thee,
Must at the side-scene make her entrances,
Or move 'neath groves cut by the carpenter;
Her song-bird is an orchestra—her stars
The stage-lights; knowing nought of seasons, but
As shown by bill or prompter's calendar;
Her seasons are theatrical—her fruits,
Her flowers, spring not from Nature's treasury,
But make-believes—peaches of wood and wax;
Not from the green-house, David, but the Green-room!
Beauty!" stormed he, "i'faith, when saw'st thou it,
Save through the tube of operatic glass?"
At which, indignant, Garrick turned aside
And left the Doctor victor.

REYNOLDS.

Pooh! mere stuff,
The loveliest women born have trod the stage!

GOLDSMITH.

But, after all, who knows *what Beauty is?*
Is it a type of feeling, fancy-like?
A question of localities—of shores?—

Of nationalities ?—To Caffre's eye
The Black is beautiful.

REYNOLDS.

                    And why not Black?
Of the Ideal, BEAUTY is the centre:—
Imagination, genius, feeling, passion,
Pay homage to the greatness there enshrined.
Art seeks to penetrate the inner veil
Where beauty sits concealed, but oftener fails
Than finds the hidden labyrinth to her feet.
Every creation of victorious Art
But vibrates to that centre; finest tones
But echo that interior harmony;
The loveliest conception doth but shape
A feeble image of the beauty shrined
Within that vast ideal . . . .

GOLDSMITH.

                          This for Art:
Yet simpler illustration may be found.

REYNOLDS.

Ever the old question, " What is Beauty ? "
You say, as thousands say, a presence fair,
Of easy elegance, elastic step,
As bounding as the sparkling foot of Spring ;

Expression that takes captive every grace,
And glads the sense to gaze, as though the world
Narrowed its orb to where one being moved,
And all the rest were barren! If 'twere thus,
Then to be thus were sure to be admired:
But there's a charm the gazer's self must find
Within himself, a portion of his life—
His own conception, feeling, sentiment,
Or Beauty's power is wanting. Some affect
A slender, delicate, half-girlish form,
Which fills them with a dream of loveliness,
Of purity, and maiden innocence;
Others select a full, round, regal shape,
Reflecting some ideal of their own,
Some Juno of their heart's mythology,
And slenderness is silliness to them!

GOLDSMITH.

'Tis true,
Each loving heart hath in its central core
Some fair imaginary sketch, some shape,
Some dream angelic of the bride to be,
Some unknown wonder, which shall yet appear;
Crossing the travel of their daily life
Find they but one, *one* charm, of those conceived
And shaped within—*their eyes create the rest!*

They see, in fact, what others cannot see;
And what seems " plain " to cold, unloving eyes,
To those that love, enzone beatitude.
As there is music which awakes no chord
Within some breasts, all perfect though it be,
So is there Beauty which affects us not,
While plainer faces thrill us with a joy
Unfelt, unimaged, unbelieved before!
Who can interpret, then, what Beauty is?

REYNOLDS.

Woman's a riddle—Beauty is the same.

GOLDSMITH.

To me,—nay, do not laugh,—in sooth, to me
There is a spirit in creation which
Seems cognizant of Art! The woodland stream
Ripples its sylvan course by mead and rock,
By nest of moorland lark, by park of deer,
Or sedgy nook, that would a painter choose;
The smallest flower that decks the hem of Spring
Seeks, as by instinct, some romantic spot,
Some shady slope, to dress its beauty in.
Earth closely knits in universal Art
The commonwealth of seasons, and their change;
Nature, a colourist—supreme as truth—
Paints with a pencil dipped in setting suns!

REYNOLDS.

You sail in Fancy's barque, and touch on shores
Seen by the dreamer's eye :—beware the rock !

GOLDSMITH.

Nay, dream it is not;—but a certainty !
The wild rose climbs the gate, or slyly seeks
Some old white gable to display herself ;
Conscious of contrast, or, in playful mood,
Toys with the sun, and kisses her own shade.

REYNOLDS.

Why, this is sketching !—you've a soul for Art.

GOLDSMITH.

From youth I grew a lover of that light
Which warms the altar of " the Beautiful ! "
I loved Mythology ; for it to me
Was the religion of the Beautiful !
But Thought is ever in advance of Action,
Could we achieve what we in thought perceive,
Then Greatness were a step of easy reach !

REYNOLDS.

Within the mind of man there glows a fire
Which hath its source from some diviner orb
Than warms our world—spark of a higher sphere ;

There, in its full integrity, exists
What we may term, for lack of better name,
The " Central Form "—the principle of Taste.
'Tis *this* that to the flagging fancy gives
Sense of a nobler mark—something beyond
What it hath yet achieved—some loftier step
Than it hath yet ascended : promptly as
This " Central Form " exerts its influence,
So its possessor moveth on to Fame ;
Retaining this, in its divine perfection,
No man, no artist, actor, sculptor, bard,
Can rest content with failure : no, 'tis this,
This inward sense of something *unachieved,*
Felt, vaguely seen, and difficult of aim,
Upward invites us, till the mounting mind
Catches the light that can immortalise !—
This sudden power, not in itself a thought,
Yet aye compelling thought ;—not Beauty, but
Extracting it ; that Beauty unto which
Each particle of universal life
Is more or less related :—this is *Genius,*
Or 'tis the *guide* of Genius—'tis the Judge
That, though *reproving,* still encourageth !
You are an artist, every poem shows—
Simple, descriptive, earnest, full of grace
And manly tenderness ; your pen excels

The painter's pencil; surely then you feel
That inward sense of something unperform'd,
Which yet your thought may grasp with diligence!

GOLDSMITH.

Conscious full often am I of a charm
In word or thought which yet I fail to reach;
And can believe it may be thus with Art.
Paintings! how they lead the mind to nature,
Inspire the spirit, lift the thought to God!—
All that in woman's life is beautiful,
All that is innocent and sweet in childhood,
All that is high, heroic, great in man!
Of fancy and reality—of taste
And truth—of glory and enthusiasm :—
How they illuminate the life of life!
Paintings to me are Prophets of Advancement!

REYNOLDS.

Poet thou art—and Nature form'd thee such;
But all too wild a spirit for that art
Where Judgment, more than Fancy, sits and acts.
Who wins must labour! not await the hour
Of some descending vision, some fair muse,
Seen in the dreams of foolish votaries.
To know one's object, and to learn the mode
Of reaching best that object; profiting

By every study ancient Art hath left;
By contemplation, and laborious zeal;
These, humble as they show and poor in sound,
Have royal right to epithets divine!
These will achieve what Dreamers ne'er achieve,
Led by the hope of some propitious star!
Some power, not won by labour, but a gift!
Alas, these *gifts,* how many a churchyard tells
Of broken hearts, of tears, of blighted homes!
The Halls of Fate are crowded by the Gifted;
The very dust is consecrate to woes,
Which found their birth in the insane belief
That untaught genius wins a world's renown,
Labour in Art scorn'd as mechanical:
Would that my voice each ardent youth might reach,
Who by his parent's table draws and dreams
Of heaven-born genius and the stars of Fame.
The only spirit worth the listening to,
Is that which bids men Work!—toil, study, learn.
This, Inspiration flouts as something low,
Unworthy her diviner attributes!

GOLDSMITH.

All men are not alike; whether it be
In brain or blood, in muscle or in nerve.
A power, to man inexplicable, still

Infuses nature ; pulses of a life
As yet unveil'd : nay, hath not temperament,
Organisation, something still to do
With those emotions which translation seek
In Art, Invention, Sculpture, Poetry?
Thoughts come uncall'd for, and exert a power
Of which we are the servants, not the master.
Some hearts can vibrate to the simplest chord,
Others an orchestra may fail to rouse.
Beauty? It dwells in Truth, in Goodness, Grace :
Beauty is mental more than physical !
You laugh, you think not thus ?—now, what's amiss?

REYNOLDS.

Keep that, my Goldie, for some future verse.

Enter SERVANT.

So please you, Sir, the little girl attends
You met with strawberries, and bade to call.

REYNOLDS.

Strawberry Girl,—well, let her call at ten.
       [*Exit Servant.*

GOLDSMITH.

The Strawberry Girl, pray let me see her.
I have a tenderness for childish life :
A man—yet something of a child myself.

Imagination builds her paradise
Deep in the wondering nature of a child :
The great, the wise, heroic, fortunate,
How shine they in the books that childhood reads !
There is a land but known to children's feet,
Wherein grow flowers that never bloom elsewhere ;
As some child-angel, passing by, had thrown
The garment of her glory over earth !
Birds sing therein, whose notes, we know, were brought
From groves by fairies haunted ; brooklets flow
In music such as heard Aladdin, when,
Full to the lips, in fortune he returned !
Oh, joy, to tread the ground of child-romance !

REYNOLDS.

Come, see the girl, and tell your story out,
Or write a book—a second Blue Beard tale,
A Cinderella, or new Riding Hood ;
Some other story of a Wondrous Lamp !
Something to rank with Giants of the Past !

[*Exeunt,* REYNOLDS *bantering.*

GAINSBOROUGH.

Scene—*The room of an old-fashioned house in Sudbury.*

Enter young Gainsborough, *with his mother, speaking earnestly.*

GAINSBOROUGH.

Well, but, dear mother, I dislike these looms—
Treddles and shuttles, steaming vats and stoves.

MRS. GAINSBOROUGH.

Speak with respect, dear boy, and quietly.

GAINSBOROUGH.

I would not hint a feeling otherwise
Than kind, and most respectful to my sire;
Others, however, may have feelings too.

MRS. GAINSBOROUGH.

Forget your feelings, and remember fortune.
Think what a life of industry may yield,—
Wealth to command the highest influence;
Wealth to assist the poor—to raise the weak;
To be a benefactor and a friend
Unto the town that bred you! *That* were well!

GAINSBOROUGH.

But to inhale the sickly breath of crowds;
Exchange the fresh glad breeze of early morn
For the close atmosphere of carded wool;
Sweet Nature's quiet face, for the quick whirl
And everlasting din of shafts and wheels!
No; Nature's manufactory for me:
She moves on silently, though reproducing
Faster than man, with all his new-found helps.

MRS. GAINSBOROUGH.

Your brother Humphrey would not argue thus.

GAINSBOROUGH.

Make Humphrey, then, the weaver; let him be
The right hand of my father; let his name
Continue on the trade of " crapes " and " says."
I'll carve out fortune with my palette knife;

A brush shall be my engine; and for steam,
For *steam*, I'll get up perseverance—yes,
High-pressure perseverance. I'll not fail!
Never believe I'll fail.

MRS. GAINSBOROUGH.

Consider this :
A tenth-rate fortune is a thing to prize;
A tenth-rate reputation—what is that ?

GAINSBOROUGH.

But I'll be first !—

MRS. GAINSBOROUGH.

First ?—my poor boy—be first ?

GAINSBOROUGH.

I will work out the poetry of Art;
Make painting read as easily as a book ;
Illustrate life and the intents of life ;
Bid Nature sit for likeness of herself,
And fix the evanescent, by a wand
Potent as young Aladdin's. You will see !
My colours, these poor colours, shall be actors,
And with each day's performance bring me fame.
Kings, queens, and nobles, warriors, ministers,
Shall tread the stage, and keep it with applause.

The world itself shall be my theatre !—
Mother, there is a bond between us twain
Which makes affection but one common pulse
Guiding two hearts—'tis *instinct*, some would say :
Mother, there is an instinct to be great—
And that I feel !—throbbing each ardent pulse,
Coursing my veins as if to win the goal.
Can Nature err who thus reveals herself?

MRS. GAINSBOROUGH.

Your father's disappointment—think of that !

GAINSBOROUGH.

He'll not be disappointed—or, if so,
But for a time—a very little time.
What is this wealth, of which he talks so much ?
Death, that can make even a Crœsus poor,
Cannot deprive the artist of his gains !
No man hath more than a life-interest
In what his toil amasses. Death stays all,
Nothing he taketh with him : not so *Fame*—
It lends a halo even to the tomb,
Crowns the dead brow, honours the lifeless hand,
Enrobes the mortal with immortal worth :—
Death cannot rob the artist of his due,
For it enricheth e'en his very dust !

And for his life—think of his glowing life!
To linger in the light of golden eves;
Take lessons of the clouds, the streams, the hills;
Ramble 'mid woody rocks and winding glades;
To watch the panorama of the roads,—
The rustic cart to distant market bound,
The harvest waggon on its rumbling way,
Children beneath the hedgerow gathering haws,
The ploughman and his team, or tripping lass
With wicker basket and her weekly eggs.
All country pictures have a charm for me!
The sheep that spot the mead, like drifting snow;
The lowing kine within the sedgy pool;
Crows wandering home before the dusk of eve;
The aged woodman shelt'ring from the storm;
Even the shepherd dog, by meadow gate,
Waiting some well-known footstep, are enough
To fill my mind with pictures yet to be!

MRS. GAINSBOROUGH.

Manhood succeeds to youth—and manhood sighs
To find youth's world a dream! Could I but think
Thy way were sure!

GAINSBOROUGH.

            Be sure I'll bring you fame;
My name shall be an honour to your years,

And, as you walk, people that pass shall say,
That is the mother of young Gainsborough.
Oh! what a joy, some day to hear you own,—
But once my son proved backward to my wish;
But once—and after that no son more true;
My wish rose not so high as he did mount.
Fame then how sacred—how divinely dear—
How doubly welcome, if my mother's heart
But share the harvest which her son hath won!
Could I yet live to hear you own at last—
My son, your choice *was right!* You were my hope;
But now you are my pride!

MRS. GAINSBOROUGH.

You are my pride!
And GOD make good your hope.

[*She falls on his neck, weeping.*

HAYDON.

(THE TWO EXHIBITIONS.)

Scene—*A room in the Egyptian Hall, Piccadilly, engaged by* Haydon *for the exhibition of his two important pictures, " The Banishment of Aristides," and " The Burning of Rome."*

HAYDON.

The world may say I've fail'd; I have *not* fail'd:
If I set truth 'fore men they will not see,
'Tis they who fail, not I. My faith holds firm,
And time will prove me right; meantime I feel
As martyrs feel who suffer for the Truth !
Art should illustrate principle; give strength
To virtue; lift the soul to God ! It claims
A higher, nobler province than to deck
The walls of lordly owners ; than to be
Mere furniture for mansions. Art—High Art—

Should foster the intelligence of nations,
Commemorate the loftiest deeds of man!

Enter LADY ETHGROVE *and* PARTY.

LADY ETHGROVE.

La, bless me, not a creature—I declare;
How vastly awkward—'tis a change, indeed,
To leave the General for Mr. Haydon.

PARTY.

A change, indeed; but surely you'll not stay?

LADY ETHGROVE *to* HAYDON.

You see I've call'd,—I promised you I'd call.
The pictures?—ah, I see;—how forcible!
Especially "The Burning,"—or, in fact,
I scarce know which is best, both are so good.
The Banishment of . . . Let me see the bill—
Of Aristides—hum!

HAYDON.

           Contemptible! (*aside.*)
Your ladyship, I fear me, hurried here
From metal more attractive—General Thumb?

LADY ETHGROVE.

Oh, such a treasure, such a little dear!
Ladies were off'ring guineas for a kiss.

HAYDON.

Indeed!

LADY ETHGROVE.

So said: though, 'faith, I offer'd none.
Charm'd as I am, I must perforce away.
These pictures quite enamour me; but still . . .

HAYDON.

Your ladyship prefers the General.
[*Walks about.*

Enter LORD LOVEL.

LADY ETHGROVE.

Ah, my Lord Lovel, have you seen the " rage,"
The wonder of the world?—so perfect, too,
From crown to heel a miracle of form!

LOVEL.

A miracle?—wherever to be seen?

LADY ETHGROVE.

General Tom Thumb—you must, indeed, go *there;*
The whole world's hurrying *there;* nothing is heard
But sayings, doings, speeches of Tom Thumb!

LOVEL.

Dwarfs suit not with my humour: when I pay
'Twill be for seeing giants, not for dwarfs.

    [HAYDON *stops in his walk and regards* LORD LOVEL.

LADY ETHGROVE.

You'll go, I know; come, see him for yourself.
Say yes—but "yes"—and straight we will return;
Though, 'faith, we've spent the whole long morning
    there.

LOVEL.

Excuse me; nothing less than man gigantic!
Not an inch less than nine full measured feet
Would tempt me to attend.

LADY ETHGROVE.

                Ah, you but jest!—
You'll see—you'll change your mind—we go with
    crowds:
Where fashion is, there go the fashionable!
And 'tis the fashion to admire Tom Thumb.
Adieu! I'm sure you'll go—quite sure you'll go.

    [*Exeunt* LADY ETHGROVE *and* PARTY.

LOVEL *to* **HAYDON.**

You seem annoy'd—yet wherefore thus annoy'd?

What need to fret at mere frivolity?
If weak, 'tis harmless, and not worth a thought.

HAYDON.

Not quite so harmless as your lordship deems.
This puny prodigy—this wondrous mite—
This dwarf—this minikin—this scrap of flesh—
This turnip-radish of a man, attracts
In myriads, while I gain in units.
Last week twelve thousand hurried to the show—
One hundred honour'd *me* with their regard:
Twelve thousand to one hundred—desperate odds!

LOVEL.

Your name and service will survive the time;
You are the prophet of a new Art-creed;
It taketh years to inculcate the " New "—
The " Old " had its believers ere we came,
And will have when we're gone.

HAYDON.
                    In fact, this world's
A riddle, and success an epigram.
Forty-two years I've battled for the cause,
Through harassments, anxieties, and loss—
And what is the result?

LOVEL.

A great result; and greater yet to come.
The Elgin Marbles gave fresh force to Art,
And your impassion'd advocacy made
Them known and loved, when scorn'd and misconceived.

HAYDON.

Kindly remark'd, my lord; spoke all like *you*,
My heart—and more, my *home*—had suffer'd less.

LOVEL.

The years to come shall pay for sorrows past;
Meanwhile, let patience minister to peace!

HAYDON.

The years to come! I hear the knell of Hope
Dolefully ringing 'neath the spectral veil
Which hides the future! In my dreams I hear
Nothing but dirges. Hope loves *youth*, not age!

LOVEL.

Some pulse of Goodness centres in all life;
Open the door, and let the Angel enter.

HAYDON.

Goodness! the revelation of GOD's love;
Yes; I have faith in *goodness*, though unfound!

And equal faith in evil influence!
No man more earnestly beseecheth GOD
For strength in weakness, for support in grief,
For aid to finish greatly what his mind
Greatly conceives, than I. Ere canvas find
A line upon its surface, my heart's prayer
Ascends to Him who is the help of all!
To Him who grasps eternity, and holds
All nature in the hollow of His hand.
Then in such mood, I feel that I could seize
E'en Samson by the throat, and conquer him!
Nothing's too vast, too high, too difficult:
I walk the level of colossal thought,
And mate with heroes in the world of Art.

LOVEL.

Proceed; I'm all attention.

HAYDON.

For a time,—
This for a time; but other moods take place:
The glory narrows to a final speck,
And darkness, thick as Erebus, succeeds:
Out of this mist of horror comes a breath—
A whisper—scarce a voice—a small thin tone
That shakes me like a reed, and makes the air

Quiver as if with dread. I try to think
Of home, of children, all endearing things
That gladden labour through the task of life;
But still that breath grows hotter in mine ear;
The darkness thickens, and an *utterance*,
More dread than any *presence* man ere saw,
Chafes my roused spirit into hate and scorn!
Infects me with a pride beyond all pride,—
Intense disdain—unequall'd arrogance—
Unmatch'd assumption of transcendent powers.
Ambition, vast as was the Morning Star's
Ere quench'd in night, possesses every nerve.
I feel the world would crush me, if it could,
But that its malice lacks the needful might:
And then I brave the worst it can perform—
Mock its opinions—crucify its idols—
Unmask its falsehoods, and expose its shams—
Counters that would be coins—mere dross for dupes!
All tongues against me—I against all tongues!
Till life appears a mesh, from which to 'scape
Were paradise—and then . . . . .
I dare not think what then!

LOVEL.

'Tis but the penalty of shatter'd nerves—
O'erwrought imagination. You need rest,

Freedom and relaxation : quit the town,
And pass a month with me at Loveltower.
Let Nature turn physician, and prescribe
As only Nature can, whose power's supreme.

HAYDON.

There's a prescription every one must take,
Sooner or later, and that sombre draught
With me seems close at hand—a grave-like phial !

LOVEL.

Come, come, be glad; discard this monkish mood.
Nature's a queen, whom GOD himself hath crowned :
Grace, Beauty, Sweetness, are her maids of honour ;
They bear her train, rich with the vernal gold
And diamonds of the morn ; and forth she moves
With Pow'r and Grandeur for her ministers :
A thousand servants wait upon her steps,
And kings are her retainers ! Come, we'll change
This scene for one of peaceful, woodland life.
I'll be the prompter, at whose magic call
Prisons are changed to palaces. You'll return
Strong to achieve; and Fame will banquet you !

HAYDON.

Fame is a myth—a ghost that wanders ruins !
A phantom that deceives, misleads, and mocks ;

What sorcery compels me to pursue
This vision?

LOVEL.

   Fame is the star of Labour,
Without it effort dies—existence pines.
Fame, or the hope of Fame, hath led to deeds
Which elevate the world,—say nought 'gainst Fame;
Fame is to Mind what Love is to the Heart,
The goddess of its worship, and its wealth:
You have no heresy 'gainst Love, we hope?

HAYDON.

Love is the law of all things visible;
From Love doth emanate the beautiful;
And from the god-like beautiful springs Form—
Form, the exponent of all majesty!

LOVEL.

We carry beauty and proportion with us;
The visual eye asks guidance from *within*,
And as that cometh is its power increased.
Some men see form the first, the colour next:
Mere outline hath to them a grander charm
Than harmony of tone or grace of hue.
Others would sit unquiet if there hung

A picture out of square, and forthwith rise,
Compell'd by impulse to adjust it right.

HAYDON.

Taste is the gold of life, where'er 'tis seen,
Though but in cottage-home, it lends a light
Not wealth itself, if wanting taste, can match.
Art, as a teacher and a benefactor,
As yet is unacknowledged: give me rule,
And Schools of Art I'd raise in every town.

LOVEL.

You pause.

HAYDON.

   The wheels fast rolling to Tom Thumb!
Hear you the inmates hurrying to the scene?
They crush—they scream—they faint. Your Lordship finds
The number here needs no arithmetic!

LOVEL.

Methought you had forgotten " such small deer ! "

HAYDON.

Who feels for *others* can forget no step
By which their happiness may be involved:
Failure in this neglected exhibition
May bring down desolation upon those

I'd gladly die to serve. But wherefore grieve?
'Tis but one heartache more! Let me proceed.

LOVEL.

Schools of Design, you say . . .

HAYDON.

Had I the means,
Schools of Design I'd build in every town;
Make Art an element of education
Common to all—the lowliest born of man;
A new community should spring around,
Refined, improved, advanced in social worth;
" Design " ere long would forth reveal itself
In every mercantile, industrial craft;
Iron and wood, nay, e'en the potter's clay,
Would offer forms of elegance and taste.
A graceful style adds nothing to the cost;
'Tis odds if *more* material be not used
To mould the vulgar than the graceful form!
A *saving!* there's attraction in the word,
Could I but prove this to the Government:
What say you?

LOVEL.

Simply this—petition Peel.

HAYDON.

I have; and he most courteously declines.
Yet Peel means well, and has a heart to feel;
Would fain do right, and yet is slow to act.
Melbourne but shrugs, and shakes his laughing sides,
And says, " What need to paint the House of Lords?
Many might say too much Art there already!
Schools of Design? What, *more* designing men?
Call you this, Haydon, serving well your country?"
So, with a joke, he laughs at argument,
And quits the question.

LOVEL.

We'll not quit it thus;
Assistance shall be had, and now, for once,
Close doors, and come with me: I have a scheme
Perchance may make a fortune; meanwhile, deem
My house a debtor by your sojourn there.

HAYDON.

Had not your lordship better ask Tom Thumb?
If *he* were absent—*I might then succeed!*

LOVEL.

The river of success runs ever clear!
All flock to see what all can understand.

If I read Shakspere, it is plain to sense,
I read to what's Shaksperian in the man.
If he be wanting in dramatic taste,
I might as well harangue the Monument!
Come, staying here doth but embitter thought.
Nay, cease to hesitate.

    HAYDON.

      Embitter thought?
Thrice happy they whose expectation's small,
And hope but little, if they hope at all!

          [Exeunt.

NOTES.

From T. Taylor's Life of Haydon.

"Advertisement. — Haydon's New Pictures. — On Easter Monday next will open for exhibition at the Egyptian Hall, Piccadilly (admission 1s., catalogues 6d.), two large pictures, viz., 'The Banishment of Aristides, with his Wife and Children,' to show the injustice of democracy; 'Nero Playing with his Lyre while Rome is Burning,' to prove the heartlessness of despotism.

"April 4th. It rained the whole day. Nobody came except Jerrold, Bowring, Fox Maule, and Hobhouse. Twenty-six years ago the rain would not have prevented them, but now it is not so. However, I do not despair.—6th. Receipts, 1846, £1 1s. 6d.; Aristides. In God I trust, Amen.—7th. Rain. £1 8s. 6d.—8th. Fine. Receipts—worse, £1 6s. 6d.—13th. Easter Monday. O God! bless my receipts this day for the sake of my creditors, my family, and my Art, Amen. Receipts (22). £1 2s.; catalogues (3) 1s. 6d.; £1 3s. 6d.

"They rush by thousands to see Tom Thumb (exhibiting in another room in the same building). They push, they fight, they scream, they faint, they cry help and murder! and oh! and ah! They see my bills, my boards, my caravans, and don't read them. Their eyes are open, but their sense is shut. It is an insanity, a rabies, a madness, a furor, a dream!"

LEONARDO DA VINCI.

LEONARDO DA VINCI.

Scene—*Gallery of Paintings in the Palace of Fontainebleau; a flight of steps descending to the garden.*

Enter Raimondi, Filippo, *and* Ginevra.

RAIMONDI.

Seven hundred crowns a year! Well, Fortune's son
Improves upon his early heritage.

FILIPPO.

A welcome boon—worthy the generous hand
And kingly heart of Francis. A wise gift!

RAIMONDI.

So after time may say: but hold you not
More than a common interest in this act,
Knowing Da Vinci long?

FILIPPO.

    From childhood, Sir.
I am ten years his senior. Neighbours' sons

Were we—wild, rambling, thoughtless, truants oft.
Val d'Arno, and the mountain tracts beyond,
Beheld us link'd together dawn and eve.
Bright days were those, Raimondi; bright but brief—
Scenes that have passed to sounds—mere things of air—
Voices that have no echo, save a sigh:
Little remains to bid us now rejoice.
Pleasure finds many doors, and knocks full loud;
She hath her *youthful* comrades as of yore:
AGE from the casement views her tripping by,
Calling no more as erst she used to call;
Singing no more as she was wont to sing!

RAIMONDI.

Well, Leonardo is advancing, too.

FILIPPO.

Genius counts days by deeds! Him I remember—
A handsome, gifted, earnest, active youth:
There was persuasion in his honest look;
None saw him but to love him.

GINEVRA.

Love him—a madcap! Sooth, I lov'd him not—
A giddy, hare-brained, noisy, reckless lad,
Ever in mischief! Never imp alive
Contrived to plague me as that rogue Da Vinci.

RAIMONDI.

I knew him when such school-day sports had ceased,
When thought made thin his cheek, when full of
    hope,
Full of the painter's ardour—young and warm,
Trembling with aspirations yet untold,
He loved to stand and gaze, full hour by hour,
Upon a Giotto or a Masaccio :—
Hearing no tongue save that which stirr'd the soul
With restless promptings unto noble deeds ;
Seeing a vision canvas never showed
Lying beyond, apart, and far above
The painted scene on which he seemed to gaze—
A world wherein dwelt name, position, fame !—
Oh, hope of Genius, how divine the air
Which wraps thy presence—how intense the joy
That agitates the step that seeks renown !

FILIPPO.

Gladsome it is to mark a gifted mind
Step from a lot, by circumstance confined,
Narrowed by poverty, and in pure force
Of self-reliant, honourable will
Make circumstance give way,—and the steep path
Which leads to station, dignity, and power,

Take, as 'twere native to the soul within,
A spirit born to climb *and to ascend!*   [*A pause.*
Oh! golden city of the land of Hope,
What hast thou not in store for those who strive
And toil, and mount, and wrestle for the wreathes
Whose leaves are—

RAIMONDI.

What?

FILIPPO.

Worthless, me thought to say;
But I am old, and aged eyes wax dim.

RAIMONDI.

And yet I've seen them gladden when thou spak'st
Of the *first* painting Leonardo wrought—
His famed Medusa . . . .

FILIPPO (*with excitement*).

Think, my Raimondi—in a low-built room—
On scrap of common wood—with clay and paint,
Of which as yet he'd scarcely learnt the use,—
Without a friend to cheer, to aid him on,
Or whisper courage,—silent and alone,
Unfriended, unassisted,—he sent forth

A work whose novelty, whose force and depth,
Astonished Florence!
     Then his modest worth;
His noble person,—handsome countenance—

GINEVRA.

A little louder speak,—I'm somewhat deaf.

FILIPPO.

A handsome lad—

GINEVRA.

Ay, ay, a franksome lad—a ne'er-do-well;
I often said he 'd never come to good.
Always devising—ever constructing,
Making, unmaking;—doing, undoing;—
Mills, bridges, boats, and other carpentry—
Leaving *a litter*, which he called " INVENTION."
Out on Invention!—'tis untidy work—
Keeps a house dirty, slovenly and rough . . .

RAIMONDI (*interrupting her*).

You'd need to speak more fittingly of one
So high in worth, in honour, as our Painter!

GINEVRA.

Painter, forsooth!—and where 's the good of it?
What 's the end of it? Who profits by it?

Painting? efecks! give me a Pantry, Sir!—
Sketching, say you—Kitchen, say I; *Kitchen!*—
The Light of Genius—can you see by it?
The Fire of Genius—can you cook with it?
What hath his genius done?

RAIMONDI.

Created works that will outlast thy grave;
A plate from one such work were worth a *sum*.

GINEVRA.

Plates, marry, plates! give me good dinner plates!
Burnished like silver, glittering in a row,
Making a dark place light;—Painting! mere stuff!
The painting on a clock but spoils the dial;
'Twould better go without it;—*Painting! Plates!*
Leonardo's a fool.   [*Exit, grumbling.*

FILIPPO.

That woman would speak evil of a saint,
As obstinate as . . . .

RAIMONDI.

What?

FILIPPO.

An old woman!—

RAIMONDI.

Mere prejudice, my Filippo, mere cant;—
True obstinacy is *young* as oft as old;
As often seen in ringlets as in wigs;
As firmly sits upon a snowy brow
As though it found ten wrinkles for a seat;
Speaks with smooth lip as boldly as with rough;
Ascribes a hundred motives for an act,
Not one of which is temper, passion, spleen.
No 'faith, 'tis "proper pride,"—'tis a "self-respect,"—
A rightful spirit suffering things unjust;
A brave resolve not to be " trampled on ! "
Your true-born stubbornness is something great;
A mixture of the martyr and the saint !—

FILIPPO.

The world hath sat in judgment and declared . .

RAIMONDI.

Tut, tut!
The world must then reverse its law.
The old? no, no!—the stubborn are *the young!*
Twenty things granted cannot make them grateful;
One thing denied sufficeth to provoke them;
The young . . It galls me to the quick . . . .

FILIPPO.

Ha! ha!
A Preacher of "*submission*" losing patience!
But of Ginevra, who has just retired,
Nothing seems right to her distorted view;
Why sent Da Vinci for her?

RAIMONDI.

Doubtless to render service; place her well;
Where her old age might meet with fitting care.
E'en I have much to thank his friendship for.
No favour promptly offer'd to his youth
Escapes his heart—eludes his memory;
The hand that did him kindness when a boy—
That hand, if needing help, he thrice repays.

FILIPPO.

God bless him for it!
           See, Da Vinci comes.

RAIMONDI.

And with the King.

FILIPPO.

'Twere better to retire.

RAIMONDI.

Two Kings:—
One has his throne within this realm of France;

The other, crown'd by Fame, ascends a throne
Acknowledged by all peoples, and all realms.

FILIPPO.

Still so enamour'd : *one* may bend the knee
To kingly worth—a *thousand* unto Kings
Without the worth ! Still nearer they approach.
We may offend.
    [*They descend the steps leading to the garden.*

Scene II.—*Enter* Francis the First *and* Leonardo.

LEONARDO.

Your Majesty outvalues much my skill.

FRANCIS THE FIRST.

Nay, good Da Vinci—not a jot too much :
Kings find few pleasures half so pure or high
As those true Art invites them to partake ;
'Tis pleasant to seek refuge from the cares,
Inquietudes, and vanities of state,
Within a world where *talking* is unknown :—
A world whose star hath set—whose day hath gone ;
Whose rank and power, whose pomp and arrogance
Are painted visions hanging 'gainst a wall !—
'Tis something to behold a human face

F

That asks not office, favour, or control,—
Here, conquests, glories, spoils, ambitions, all
Shrink into silence ;—beauty lifts her gaze,
In immortality of loveliness,
Yet craves nor title, pension, nor reward :
Sworn foes frown face to face, yet draw no sword ;
The envious cease their scandals ; and the false
Have done with stratagems and low *finesse.*
Oh, World of Art, thou dost rebuke the life
We prize so much, yet pass so peevishly !
Say, my Da Vinci, what drew first thy thought
Unto this sphere of thy divinity ?
Art, we remember, was thy second choice.

LEONARDO.

In youth my great ambition was the Muse ;—
To leave a poem that might shrine my name
For centuries ; to represent the mind,
The spirit, manners, progress of the Age ;
To pioneer the path to higher aims
And holier aspirations,—to advance
The Arts and Science of my country,—these—
These were the thoughts that, like unbearing trees,
Show'd many leaves, but never came to fruit :—
A few light sonnets, a few passing songs,
And the strings jarr'd, and all again was mute.

FRANCIS.

Some sonnets we have seen, yet scarce regret
The Poet lost for the true Painter found.

LEONARDO.

Ah, my liege—
Some hundreds enter the wide boat of Fame,
But in few years Time throws full many out ;—
Pass half a century, and half remain ;—
A hundred years, and you may count their heads
By twos and threes—the multitudes are gone :
And still the Immortal City shines afar ;
Still longer centuries must intervene
Ere on that coast to Genius consecrate
The Pilgrim's name may live for evermore,
Writ high above the casualties of time !—
Such height, I fear, my name may never reach.

FRANCIS.

Great men know not their greatness—'tis the air,
The daily element, which they respire ;
Greatness is *habitude,* and strikes them not !

LEONARDO.

My next ambition was to cope with Time ;—
Anticipate the future, and invent
Machines that should achieve what human hands,

By tens of thousands, could not execute;
To bring the poor cheap bread, and better garb,
Healthier homes, and life at lesser cost;
And partly 'twas accomplish'd;—my next step,—

FRANCIS.

And best—

LEONARDO.

Would I could think so; but, my liege,
What yet is done seems small to the " to be "—
That grows, enlarges—but 'tis ever so:
The *prize* of time is in the years to come,
The time we have we prize not!—

FRANCIS.

Say not so!
One work is done which every heart must prize!
Art is the bridge that leads from years of time
To the eternal years whose sun is Fame!
To speak not of the female heads thy skill
Hath dower'd with beauty and perpetual grace,
Whose tender playfulness, expression, power;
Whose *purity*, refinement, breathe a life—
A stamp of truth, unequall'd erst in Art,—
Omitting these, one great achievement stands
To guard thy name from man's forgetfulness—

One noble labour—" The Lord's Supper!" whence,
Whence rose the seed of this? A sudden thought,
Or long premeditation?

LEONARDO.

    Good, my liege,
The painting honour'd with such special praise
Was my sole thought for years :—full oft the hope
Of its accomplishment died in my breast,
Again to be renew'd—with higher zeal
And bolder impulse ; then again delay'd.
The day my hand, irresolute and slow,
Dared the *commencement* of so grand a theme,
A solemn sense of some companionship
Compell'd my pencil silently to paint ;—
Fused feeling into colours ;—soon this pass'd,
And my whole being own'd some presence gone.
Still day by day, week, month, and year, I strove;
Onward, though slow, till each Disciple's head
Before my mind, as in a mirror, came,
And lived upon the canvas as they rose ;
When each received my last, half-lingering touch,
I turned to that, which made reflection ache,
To that—*the one untouched*—all else complete :—
The head of our Redeemer—the Divine,
Incarnate Saviour,—Ransom infinite !

How dared I execute those lineaments?
With what expression might I mould that face—
That head, which God himself had glorified—
That hand which angels worshipp'd in their spheres:
That hand!—Oh, miracle of gracious love,—
Which gave itself to wounds, our souls to heal,
And lift them pure before the face of God?
I paused and wept:—what could I else but weep?
What other offering had my soul to yield
For such self-sacrifice—such love supreme?

[A pause.

FRANCIS.

Emotion is the spring of excellence;
He must feel deeply who'd make others feel.

LEONARDO.

Oh! my mind long'd—yet fear'd the wondrous theme—
To mark each scene and circumstance that left
A glory round Jerusalem—that endow'd
The everlasting tongue of love with truth,
That lifted man to an inheritance
Surpassing earthly kingdoms—made the grave
A gateway unto light!—a path o'er which
Shone the unsetting day of righteousness!
To portray Him who trod the wilderness
And held communion with eternity :—

He who loved Martha, Mary, Lazarus;—
Who on his breast received the slumb'ring brow
Of his disciple John;—whose tenderness
Broke forth in syllables that live insphered;—
Who to the universal Mother called,
With voice that thrills each matron-heart e'en now,
" Suffer little children to come unto Me!"
Oh, lips Divine—oh, words omnipotent,
Solace unmatch'd, and comfort unconceived—
How could man's pencil seek to realise
An image that could live—resembling *Thee?*
But I forget the presence of my King,—

FRANCIS.

Thy King would have thee still forget;
Proceed.

LEONARDO.

Then pass'd a vision, or perchance a dream,
I know not what, but *vision it appear'd!*
In which I seem'd *spectator*, and not actor:—
Coming and going without thought of mine—
A vision that surprised me unto tears!—
As music to the ear—so to my soul
Rang the innumerable harmonies
Of heaven, of angels, and the hosts of GOD!

FRANCIS.

We have felt painting thus ourself, Da Vinci,
As voiceless sermons—silent psalms to GOD—
Mute and yet eloquent:—they bade us feel
What words were powerless to communicate.

Enter OFFICER.

FRANCIS.

What interruption now? Who waits without?

OFFICER.

My liege, the deputies of Burgundy
Entreat an audience . . . .

FRANCIS (*aside*).

What broil's abroad?
What fresh chagrin, vexation, discontent,
Trouble our deputies? Well, 'tis some gain
To snatch an interval, though brief as this,
From frets of rule and jealousies of state.
The STATE is KING, and sovereigns are its slaves.

(*To* DA VINCI.)

You to your canvas—we to council go.
Happier *your* realm than any realm we know.

GIULIO ROMANO.

SCENE—GIULIO *in the Hall of Constantine, steadfastly regarding Raffaelle's picture of "Justice and Mercy." To him enter* DONATINI *and* FRANCESCO.

GIULIO.

Now, Donatini, what's the latest news?

DONATINI.

Cardinal Tortoso has been chosen Pope,
And with new title fills the papal chair.

GIULIO.

Adrian the Sixth—the news is six hours old!

DONATINI.

Adrian the Sixth—and further, in your ear
Let it be whisper'd,—Angelo's recall'd!

GIULIO.

Recall'd! That's news, and welcome news to Art.

BONATINI.

You fear no rival, Raffaelle being dead:
Others, less lib'ral, perchance had thought
Bad news, and most unwelcome.

GIULIO.

     Rival, no!
Art hath no rival, save unrivall'd Nature:
Each gifted mind is a new strength to Art;
New wealth, new capital; and weak is he
Who dreads a brother greater than himself.
He knows not Art, nor Art's exalted aim.

FRANCESCO.

What is the aim of Art?

GIULIO.

      It is to teach
Through power of beauty the eternal power!
It is to feel our own humanity
Enlarge with Science, to evolve out of
The perishable the imperishable!
'Tis to give feature to imagination,
Set clear the visionary forms of fancy,
Make shadows *real*, hold the fleeting *fast!*
To snatch the spark that can illuminate.

FRANCESCO.

By this we must conceive you designate
The highest order of Inventive Art;—
Nature hath other schools and colleges,
Other degrees and honours.—Is 't not so?

GIULIO.

Reigns, customs, manners change, but not so man:
The spirit of the old humanity
Invigorates the new; Man changes more
In symbol than in essence;—and the thoughts
That thrill'd Apelles in long ages back
Thrill Grecian breasts e'en now; and to the end
The grandeur and the majesty of Art
Shall wake grand thoughts, and Truth and Justice
Keep their primal state and regal dignity.

FRANCESCO.

To follow up this subject. It would seem
Art, in its highest form, hath province here
But second to religion—that is, to raise
And spiritualise our nature!—thus—

GIULIO.

Time hath made pictures *altars!* they've received
The homage vouchsafed to divinity;
It is the soul's prerogative to soar!

An impulse God implanted from the first,
When he created man : as it is nature
In the earth to feel the influence of spring,
So is it nature in the soul to feel
The influence of Art.

     DONATINI.
       Thought all like you
It might be well.

     GIULIO.
       Who 's the true patriot,
He who sets *himself* above his country,
Or he who, for that country's sake, would see
Self, power, possession—everything—forgot;
And, scorning death, with his last effort cry,
Make way for Rome, ye nations?—so with Art.

     DONATINI.
Give me your hand—right nobly said, Romano.
Less self, less thought of self, less show of self,
More thought of that which teaches love of all;
More love of that which teaches thought for all.

     GIULIO.
Ah! who so just, unenvious; who so kind
As noble Raffaelle? Oft I 've heard him say,
" *Thank* God *I breathe the air of Angelo!* "

And Angelo, whene'er he visits Rome,
Will see no spot more precious to his thought,
More touching to his heart, than the dear earth
Which wraps the form of Santi Raffaelle.

FRANCESCO.

From what dire circumstance arose the fact
That Michael, that great mark and pride of Rome,
Was forced to visit Pietra? 'Twas most strange!

GIULIO.

Leo the Tenth, whose brief pontificate
Made a new era in the world of Art,
On his accession to the papal throne
Profess'd regard for Michael Angelo;
Love for his fame, and zeal for his success;
Desired his genius for his native city;
And Angelo, as if foreboding ill,
Reluctantly obey'd the Pontiff's call.

FRANCESCO.

'Tis true; but thence to Florence order'd, forth
To build, of Saint Lorenzo, the façade.

GIULIO.

What follow'd next? 'Tis known throughout the realm,
Instead of the façade—unfinish'd yet
Since the old Cosmo time—instead of *this*,

Great work and fit for Genius to perform,
He, Michael Angelo, the soul of Art,
Was straight dismiss'd to Pietra, to decide
Between the quarries of the mountains there
And the pure marble of Carrara—thus
For eight long toilsome years he fashion'd blocks,
Constructed roads o'er marshes to the sea,
Travell'd with rafts and fascines! Believ'st thou?
He—Rome's great architect and ornament,
True Painter, Poet, Sculptor—left to toil
Like common mason—a mere blank in life;
His time consumed—his glorious talents lost
During the whole, hard reign of Leo Tenth?

DONATINI.

It mocks belief!—myriads, as yet unborn,
Will read, yet doubt; and ask, can this be true
Which wars 'gainst sense?

GIULIO.

     You saw me gazing here
On Justice and on Mercy!—shadows both:
They have no living semblances on earth!
To think of eight years in such labour spent!

DONATINI.

A loss no Pope of Rome may e'er compute:
A loss posterity will long deplore!

GIULIO.

Years, generations, empires and their crowns,
Follow each other to the end of time:
All things of earth are reproduced by earth;
Genius hath no successor!—knows no heir!—
Angelo *dead*—what centuries could replace
The grand old spirit of that master-mind?
Angelo *living*—any puny power
May cramp and fetter. Rome! it makes me mad
To think of Michael and Pietra Santé.

DONATINI.

Go where ye will, this is the fate of Genius!
Ever the stream of life is full of turns
And rough impediments; to chafe at fate
Is but to sink the deeper.

GIULIO.

    Sad as true,
The path of fame finds many a weary foot,
And aching head, and disappointed heart;
Many ascend, few reach the toilsome height!

DONATINI.

Whate'er the Present owes the Future pays!
Towards the Pantheon let us hasten now.

GIULIO.

First meet we Angelo—conduct him there;
There, 'neath its cupola, survey the tomb
Of Raffaelle:—let Genius mourn for Genius;
A tear from Michael Angelo would soothe
That spirit, call'd too early from the world,
Too early from that sphere which he adorn'd.

DONATINI.

Too early, yes; too soon for Art! and yet
That is not Death which brings not death to fame:
He lives, who leaveth an immortal name.

[*Exeunt.*

SONGS AND POEMS.

THE CHAPEL-BELL.

The wintry winds blow wild and shrill,
   Like ghosts they shriek across the moor,
Or howl beneath the window sill,
   Or shake with gusty hands the door;
And, hour by hour, from some lone bell
   A wizard sound at night doth steal—
Sometimes 'tis like a funeral knell,
   Sometimes 'tis like a marriage peal!
I know it is some fiend that stands
   Within the belfry's ghastly gloom,
And with its stark and fleshless hands
   Rings out dead souls from tomb to tomb.

I long to weep—I pray to sleep,
   But through the haunted house it sounds,
And through my flesh the chill veins creep
   Like wintry worms in burial-grounds.

A weight is on my heart—my brain,
    A shadow flits across the floor;
And then I know it is in vain
    To pine, or pray, or struggle more!
Well, let the foul fiend ring till morn—
    Till the red sun awakens men:
Yet, though thus tortured and forlorn,
    What then I did—I'd do again!

He thought it fine to feign a love
    Which woo'd my spirit to his feet;
He raised his false, false eyes above,
    And vow'd, what's useless to repeat.
Whate'er he vow'd, there is no name
    So black on earth as his deceit;
Whate'er he vow'd, there is no shame
    So vile as in his heart did beat!
Ring out, thou bitter fiend, till morn
    Awakes the prying eyes of men;
Yet prison'd, madden'd, and forlorn,
    What then I did—I'd do again!

Not slightly was I woo'd or won;
    For years the whisp'ring false one came,
And nought a saint might fear to shun
    Forewarn'd me of the villain's aim.

I loved him—loved? I would have died,
    If dying ought to him might spare;
I would have every pain defied
    To save him from a single care!
Toll, toll, thou fiend, ring out, and tell
    The murd'rous deed from goal to goal!
I know my name is writ in hell—
    I feel there's blood upon my soul!

The dawn arose, but not for me
    The bridal train did wait and smile;
As slowly, stately, three by three,
    They swept in beauty down the aisle.
I crept behind the pillar'd base;
    The bride's white garments fann'd my cheek;
The blood rush'd madly to my face;
    I dared not breathe—I could not speak!
Laugh out, thou fiend, laugh out and scorn,
    With mocking sounds, my weary ear!
Is there no other—lost—forlorn,
    No other wretch whose life's a tear?

There rose a whisper deep and low—
    A sound that took away my sight;
All things around me seem'd to flow,
    And wander in a demon light!

I nerved my hand to grasp the steel;
    I stepp'd between him and his bride.
Who'd think so black a heart could feel?—
    Could pour so warm, so red a tide?
Is there no sinful soul but mine,
    Thou endless fiend, that thou must make
These serpent sounds to hiss and twine
    Around me till my senses ache!

I had not stabb'd him, but I saw
    My noble father's thin gray hairs;
And that, perchance, which tears might draw,
    Drew blood upon me unawares.
I flung the shrieking bride apart;
    I sprang before him in his guilt;
The steel went quivering to his heart—
    Would GOD my own blood had been spilt!
Laugh out, dark fiend! beside me then
    A wilder sound than thine was spread;
A cry I ne'er shall hear again
    Till every grave gives up its dead!

Twelve months—dark months—I groan'd in pain
    A curse lay heavy on my head.
They tell me I have ne'er been sane
    Since that wild hour the bridegroom bled!

They say no shadow stalks the room—
   No midnight tolling haunts the air.
'Tis false! You hear it through the gloom :
   And, see, *the phantom* passes—there !
Mad—mad? 'Twere blissful but to lose
   One hour from self—one moment free
From thoughts that every *hope* refuse—
   From life whose lot is misery !

Mad—mad? As if the sense could leave
   The form it tortured ! Never more
Shall I do aught but rave and grieve,
   And wish—vain wish—this life were o'er !
Away!—a thousand lives have gone,
   A thousand phantoms glide in hell ;
But not one perish'd—no, not one
   So black in guilt as he who fell !
Night after night, 'mid sounds aghast,
   That fiend, that spectre, haunts my way.
What shall I see when life hath past,
   And Night is mine that knows no day ?

ENDURANCE.

I.

Ever struggle and endurance:
    "Is there no repose?" I cried;
Gives the world but this assurance,—
    Others *thus* have lived and died?

II.

On the broad highway of being
    Crowds on crowds still ever go;
Nothing more beyond them seeing
    Than to toil with foreheads low.

III.

To a spot I wander'd dreary,
    With thick branches overlaid,
For the sunlight made me weary—
    There seem'd solace in the shade.

IV.

On a bank my limbs reposing,
    Found a momentary balm;
Spirit worn, my eyelids closing,
    Sought forgetfulness and calm.

V.

Still that thought, for ever present,
    Came with purpose unexprest;
As beneath the moon's dim crescent
    Glides some ghost that cannot rest.

VI.

Seeking hint or clue to guide me,
    As I leant upon the earth,
I beheld a flower beside me
    Struggling, midst the soil, to birth.

VII.

Through the winter's wrath and rigour,
    Pent in dust, and prison'd fast,
Had it forced its path with vigour,
    Till obstruction *ceased* at last!

VIII.

Now within its emerald bosom
    All the future life reposed—
Swell'd the rich and golden blossom
    That the morn would see unclosed.

IX.

Then my heart, with sudden motion,
    Lost the weight so hard to bear;
And some new and sweet devotion
    Soothed and sanctified its care.

X.

He who thus the flower hath moulded,
    Sphered its being to this span;
He, too, hath the future folded
    In the living soul of man!

XI.

For a time the soil is round us,
    For a time we feel the thorn;
When the spirit-hour hath found us,
    Inner glories shall be born!

XII.

Welcome struggle and endurance—
   Welcome toil, to *this* allied;
Welcome the divine assurance,—
   Others thus have lived and died!

XIII.

Toil, I kiss thee with affection,
   Never more shall mortal say
That I view thee with dejection—
   That I murmur on my way.

XIV.

Through the soil and earthy ember,
   He who raised the flower from dust—
He will also man remember;
   And in Him I move and trust?

YEARS TO COME.

I.

A DAY will dawn I ne'er shall see;
    A night will set I ne'er shall know;
The wave-tide of humanity
    Thus ever surges to and fro.

II.

The dew with gems shall bead the flower,
    The bird make rich the morn with song;
And Mind, still climbing hour by hour,
    Find worlds beyond the starry throng.

III.

Years shall return to future years
    What ages unto them have given,
And that high power which Faith reveals,
    Grasp the fixed points of earth and Heaven.

IV.

The boy shall loiter through the lane,
   With school-ward footsteps short and slow;
Afraid each moment to remain,
   And yet still more afraid to go!

V.

Ah, priceless years! if boyhood knew
   The mark and value of such time;
Ah, happy school! could youth but view
   The future and its paths sublime.

VI.

What younger Howard then might feel—
   What other Wilberforce arise—
What Burke assert the general weal—
   What Rosse or Newton span the skies!

VII.

The joys, the hopes, the interests,
   That animate the bosom now,
Shall lend their glow to other breasts—
   And flush the young enthusiast brow.

VIII.

The majesty of manhood then
   May aim at some diviner worth;
And progress grant to future men
   A wider brotherhood on earth.

IX.

What theory shall then succeed?
  What deeper power—what newer theme—
What fresh discovery supersede
  The electric flash—the steed of steam?

X.

Who 'll be the bard to England dear,
  When centuries have filed and fled?
Or who the statesmen crowds will cheer,
  Worthy the Peels or Chathams dead?

XI.

The passions that distract mankind—
  The pride, the envy, and mistrust—
Shall they be scatter'd on the wind
  That lifts the banner of the just?

XII.

Shall Christian sense e'er sheathe the sword?
  Shall simple Justice rule the land?
Shall Law its shield of right afford,
  A right that all may understand?

XIII.

The languid sun fades in the sky;
  The sap within the tree droops low;
The cold wind whispers winter nigh,
  And soon the last lorn leaf must go!

XIV.

Yet he who in all change can find
    A providence of goodness shown—
He who is ruler o'er his mind
    Is more than he who rules a throne.

XV.

A day shall come I ne'er shall see,
    A day when heart and tongue lie dumb;
That day, O Lord, be Thou with me—
    And oh, on earth, Thy kingdom come!

"NIGHT" AND "MORNING."

[The title of "Night" and "Morning" is given to two excellent paintings by Sir Edwin Landseer. Few of the fine works, even of this our modern master, demand greater attention. The subject is simple in both pictures. In the first we perceive a couple of deer contending for the mastery, on an elevated piece of moorland adjoining a lake; the moon has risen above the distant hills which form the horizon. "Morning" shows to us the result of the combat—the animals are dead.]

AFAR o'er the mountains the mists are unroll'd,
And the wings of the Morn scatter crimson and gold;
The voice of the torrent is heard on its way
Proclaiming the power and the glory of day;
While each object the soul with magnificence fills,
And the heart seems to echo the joy of the hills.
What cry comes so swift from the solitude vast?
What feet sweep the glen like the rush of the blast?

'Tis the stag of the desert—the monarch whose throne
Is girt with a grandeur to cities unknown;
He was up with the dawn, over heather and fen—
Over corrie and cairn—over moorland and glen;

From bold Ben-y-chatt to Loch Diric he flew,
Nor stayed he his hoof at Glenbruar nor Chroo;
With the foam-speed of passion he bated no breath,
But away—still away—to the combat of death!

Where shrieks the lone eagle, where skulks the lean fox,
And the wolf holds her watch from her home mid the rocks;
Where the spray of the torrent is hung like a shroud,
And the pine soars aloft through the rack of the cloud:
Still onward he rushes, still bounds at a pass,
Each rugged and stern and precipitous mass;
Up, upward, he toils, by no danger deterr'd,
'Till his *rival* appears in the midst of the herd!

One glance—and together they spring o'er the path—
One moment, each eye-ball is gleaming with wrath:
Now butting, now goring—their haunches they bow:
Now tossing in fury, clash antler and brow;
'Till the fire of their passion falls faint by degrees,
And panting and foaming they sink to their knees;
Still horn linked in horn, still contending with fate,
While the moonlight looks down on their fury and hate!

But the moonlight hath gone; and the Morning hath thrown
Over mountain and river a spell of her own:—

A freshness that sparkles with heavenly light,
A beauty that glorifies hollow and height :
The gold of the summits is tinctured with rose,
And the air with a gladness and holiness glows ;
Above—springs enchantment in every breath,
Below—there's the rock—and the vulture—and death.

Who recks what that Night of contention hath seen ?
Who recks what the rage of the rivals hath been ?
As, hour after hour, gash'd and gory they stood,
From the fetlock to neck plash'd with foam and with blood,
With antlers so lock'd, that no strength could unclose
The clasp that in life they had fasten'd as foes !
Now the fox to his banquet in silence may prowl,
And the wild eagle shriek to the wolf's hungry howl.

THE BEST ESTATE.

The Heart it hath its own estate—
  The Mind it hath its wealth untold;
It needs not fortune to be great,
  While there's a coin surpassing gold.

No matter which way Fortune leans,
  Wealth makes not Happiness secure :
A little mind hath little means—
  A narrow heart is always poor.

Stern Fate the greatest still enthrals,
  And Misery hath its high compeers :
For Sorrow enters palace halls,
  And queens are not exempt from tears.

The princely robe and beggar's coat,
  The scythe and sword, the plume and plough,
Are in the grave of equal note,—
  Men live but in the eternal " Now ! "

Still Disappointment tracks the proud—
    The bravest 'neath defeat may fall;
The high, the rich, the courtly crowd
    Find there's calamity for all.

'Tis not the house that honour makes,—
    True honour is a thing divine;
It is the mind precedence takes,—
    It is the spirit makes the shrine!

So keep thou yet a generous heart,
    A steadfast and contented mind;
And not, till death, consent to part
    With that which friend to friend doth bind.

What's utter'd from the life within
    Is heard not by the life without;
There's always something to begin
    'Twixt life in faith, and life in doubt!

But grasp thou Truth—though bleak appears
    The rugged path her steps have trod—
She'll be thy friend in other spheres;
    Companion in the world of God.

Thus dwelling with the wise and good—
    The rich in thought, the great in soul—
Man's mission may be understood,
    And part prove equal to the whole!

THE BEST ESTATE.

We know not half we may possess,
    Nor what awaits, nor what attends,—
We 're richer far than we may guess.
    Rich as Eternity extends!

The Heart it hath its own estate,
    The Mind it hath its wealth untold;
It needs not fortune to be great,
    While there 's a coin surpassing gold!

IN MEMORIAM.

Day after day, the angels say,
    Innumerable souls ascend;
Day after day, we mourn and pray
    For some departed friend;
Yet never kinder heart than thine,
    And never truer breast
E'er soar'd unto a world divine,
    Or won immortal rest.

O school-companion, playmate, friend !
    I muse the long years o'er,
And weep to see the shroud descend
    Which folds thee evermore:
I shrink to yield thee to the dust—
    To mark the funeral pall;
And strive to teach my heart to trust
    In Him who feels for all !

And can it be that thou art dead,
　And I left to deplore?
I almost seem to list thy tread—
　To hear thee at the door:
The path, it was thy wont to cross,
　I gaze upon, and wait;
And scarce can realise my loss,—
　A loss so deep—so great!

Our school-days seem to dawn again;
　Again the same light beams;
A different light than falls on *men*,
　A radiance full of dreams.
The future—*what it was to be!*
　When all our hopes seem'd truth;
Alas, the things we live to see
　Are not the dreams of youth!

Is there a childhood in that sphere
　To which thy soul hath fled?
Do we begin the spirit-year,
　New-born from out the dead?
Tread we eternity at first,
　As we trod time of yore?
Or, does immortal glory burst
　At once from God's own shore?

O gate of death! O gate of life!
    O mystery sublime!
With everlasting wonders rife,
    And marvels of all time ;—
Say, shall affections still remain?
    Shall memories endure?
And links of friendship's endless chain
    Eternity secure?

Shall truth find truth, and love find love,
    Within that better world?
Shall all the tears and pains we prove
    Be ever earthward hurl'd?
Shall friend meet friend in that blest hour,
    Before their SAVIOUR's sight,
And feel that Death no more hath power
    To separate or blight?

My heart hath faith—my soul hath hope,
    Once more to see thy face;
A few brief years with time to cope,
    Then newer worlds to trace!
A few brief years on earth to roam,
    And then, when death is o'er,
Angels for friends—and Heaven for home—
    And love for evermore!

THE WANDERER.

Three dreary years in peril tost—
   Three years upon a polar sea :
Ice-wreck'd,—and half his comrades lost ;
   Once more his native land treads he.

While westward from the sandy height
   He views where, far, his cottage lies,
A father's transport fills his sight,
   A husband's joy o'erflows his eyes !

He speeds by each remember'd way,
   Each turning brings him still more near ;
He sees his first-born child at play—
   And calls—but cannot make him hear

Fast as he speeds his child appears
   Still distant as it was before ;
At length, with bursting, grateful tears,
   He sees his young wife at the door.

She takes the sweet child by the hand,
    She kisses him with loving joy;
The gazer deems in all the land
    There's no such other wife or boy!

She lifts him fondly to her cheek,
    Then leaves the narrow wicket gate;
The Wanderer thinks he will not speak,
    But gaze and wait—if love can wait!

But from that gate, to open view,
    Come never more those feet so light;
There grew no covert, that he knew,
    Whose leaves might hide them from his sight.

A sudden terror fills his veins
    And chills the rapture in his eyes;
With eager spring the gate he gains;
    And calls, but not a voice replies.

The door—it does not stand ajar—
    The casement, too, is closed and dark;
Across the path is thrown a bar—
    And all wears desolation's mark!

He shrieks in fear each name so dear—
    The garden plot is waste and wild;
O God! why doth his wife not hear?
    O love! why cometh not his child?

He strains to catch the slightest trace
    Of form or raiment; nought is seen;
As, with a wild and spectral face,
    The gray boughs groan and intervene!

The leaves bend trembling to their root,
    The frail grass mutters to the flower;
With ghost-like wing the long rays shoot,
    While tolls the bell the vesper hour.

He turns bewilder'd at the sound—
    Again his wife, his child, appear;
They move across the churchyard ground,
    And beckon the pale Wanderer near.

A few steps more and he may hold
    The twain within his trembling arms:
Why seems his sinking heart so cold?
    What shakes him with these dread alarms?

Pale, in the dreary moonlight, gleams
    Each mound and monumental stone;
He stands distraught—as one that dreams—
    Was he again alone—alone?

Alone—they've pass'd—yet nothing stirr'd!
    He thought that thro' the spectral air
There rose one low, one little word,
    Faint echo of some infant prayer!

He thought that name, which erst had mov'd
    His pulses with a parent's joy,
Came softly—as in hours beloved—
    When on his glad knee sat his boy!

Yet all had fled: and on the stone
    Beneath his feet two lines were read;
Sad lines, that to the eyes once shown,
    Do break the heart; that's better dead!

He press'd his hot lips to each name—
    He kiss'd each letter o'er and o'er—
They scorch'd his sight, as if with flame;
    They sear'd his worn heart to the core.

For this—he cried—for this was won
    My way thro' tempests!—this—to bear:
Still—still, O God—Thy will be done!
    Yet one—not one! not one to spare!

 * * * * * *

Morn stepp'd from out the mists of heaven,
    And coldly lit each hallow'd spot;
Another morn to him was given—
    Another world, where death was not!

A DAILY SCENE.

A DIM light in the window,
    Deep straw around the gate,
And silence lingering as in pain
    Some closing breath to wait.

Is it a mother that departs?
    A sire, whose course is o'er?
A child, mid tears and breaking hearts,
    That speeds to death's mute shore?

Doth friend lose friend? Some comrade old
    That early boyhood knew—
When like a lamb from Nature's fold
    Life drank the morning dew.

We know not. This alone we know;
    There is no home but tells
Some sorrow in this world below
    Of graves and funeral bells.

Some flower beloved that bloomed in vain,
　　Some joy that could not last;
Some hope that darken'd into pain;
　　Some grief that shrouds the past.

Another sun hath bathed the lawn
　　In light, and golden air;
The dead hath found another dawn,
　　A dawn which angels share.

Around the house a sadness steals,
　　A weight that pains the brow;
There is no fear of rolling wheels;
　　No need of caution now.

No need of blind-drawn windows,
　　Nor deep straw, borne aside,
To tell us in that darken'd home
　　Some heart hath loved and died.

THE VICAR'S BLIND DAUGHTER.

Lone, yet never feeling lonely,
   For her spirit peace can win;
Blind she is, but darkness only
   Dwells without, and not within.
Face of friend or brother never
   Lent their image to her eyes;
Yet the world seems kindly ever,
   And its love wears no disguise!

Let us sit awhile beside her—
   Watch her life a single day;
See the angel that doth guide her
   Gently through her darken'd way:
Nature hath but one concealment—
   All that eloquence can yield
Meets her soul in rich revealment;
   Voice of stream, and wood, and field!

E'en the Summer flowers, though lowly,
    Gather their whole heart's perfume
With a sweetness still more holy,
    As to sanctify her gloom.
Charm of hue they cannot send her;
    Yet her gentle *touch* they meet
With a softness far more tender,
    And a sweetness still more sweet.

Not a rustic in the village,
    Not a ploughman labouring nigh,
But, forgetting toil and tillage,
    Blesses her as she goes by:
She knows all the children's voices,
    Calls their young names o'er and o'er;
Every mother's heart rejoices
    As she standeth by the door.

For she feeleth for their sorrow,
    Careth for them in their care;
Helpeth them to meet the morrow
    With the little she's to spare.
In their sickness she is near them,
    In each trial of their lot
She is first to aid and cheer them;
    None in sorrow are forgot!

So she fills her daily mission
    With unwearied heart and mind,
Helping all in hard condition,
    Leaving sorrow more resign'd !
So each night, by angels tended,
    Finds she Nature's rest increase ;
And that days in duty ended
    Bring the spirit perfect peace.

Call you life like this privation ?
    Hath not GOD's own word supplied,
Ev'n in darkness, consolation—
    Joys, through JESUS, multiplied ?
Light, which earthly vision never
    Yet beheld on sea or shore,
Hopes, no darkness can dissever,
    Lift her soul for evermore !

CRADLE SONG.

Near a chin, like bank of snow,
Dwells a lip where kisses grow;
Eyes, where little angels dwell,
Each within its azure cell;
Tiny dimples in each cheek
Seem, in Fancy's ear, to speak:
So, at least, the mother sings—
Wond'ring babies have not wings!

Strange what mothers can believe;
Strange how human eyes deceive:
Nothing seem'd, as I stood by,
More than right in chin and eye.
As for infant lips, we know
Where they come, there kisses grow!
But young mothers think such things—
Fancy, babies born with wings!

THE WOODLAND WAY.

"Still day by day the woodland way,
 I wonder you 're not weary, Jane."
"I go to hear the woodlark, dear,
 And list the linnet's merry strain."
"The lark soars in the sun's warm ray,
 The linnet 's heard in every lane;
But day by day the woodland way!
 There 's sure some other reason, Jane?"

Jane turned aside with wounded pride,
 And left her friend without a look;
She knew each turn by moss and fern,
 Each narrow winding of the brook:
But still a voice *within* would say,
 A conscience-voice, that whisper'd plain,
"Still day by day the woodland way!
 There 's sure some other reason, Jane?"

Still through the glade, in light and shade,
    She wander'd far, until she found
An aged thorn,—where time had worn
    Deep rents and hollows near the ground :
There, soft and white, just hid from sight,
    A small seal'd note her fingers gain :
Ah, never bird, that love e'er heard,
    Had *note* so sweet, so dear, to Jane !

NOT MY OWN.

I TOLD my lips they must disguise
    The secret of my soul;
But oh, my heart flew to my eyes,
    And told almost the whole!

Oh, eyes too swift of love to speak,
    No more such thoughts reveal!
'Twas vain: Love next upon my cheek
    Wrote all I would conceal!

And thus, by every glance betray'd,
    My hidden love made known,
I'm of my very heart afraid,
    For it seems *not my own!*

FREAKS OF FATE.

Things congenial lose each other,
    Life and love are incomplete;
Hearts akin to one another
    Rarely are the hearts to meet!
Where's the reason? Tell me whether
    'Tis Fate's star that thus decides;
That brings opposites together,
    And the similar divides!
Spirits suited lose each other:
    Time is but a long deceit;
Hearts akin to one another
    Rarely are the hearts to meet.

Fortune seems to make alliance
    Where conformity rebels;
As in Nature's plain defiance,
    Matching where no fitness dwells!

What is this which chains existence
   To an uncongenial state?
Should the soul not make resistance
   'Gainst this tyranny of fate?
Spirits suited lose each other,
   Life and love are incomplete;
Hearts akin to one another
   Rarely are the hearts to meet.

WATCHING AND WAITING.

EVER weeping at the casement,
    Ever looking, leaning out;
While the village, in amazement,
    Wonder what this grief's about!
With the morn-light, gray and dreary,
    Long ere waketh bird or bee,
Mary stands, with spirit weary,
    Gazing out upon the sea.
There, until the w   an gl th,
    Lists she to each breeze that blows;
But the wind, though much it knoweth,
    Telleth no one what it knows,—
    No one—no one—what it knows.

On a coast forlorn, forsaken,
    Dug by hard and hasty hands,
Near a low cross, rudely shapen,
    Rests a grave upon the sands!

Never wing of bird comes near it,
    Nothing but the billows' roar ;
And a voice—the night stars hear it—
    Sighing, " Mary, never more ! "
Still, until the west sun gloweth,
    Mary lists each breeze that blows ;
But the wind, though much it knoweth,
    Telleth no one what it knows,—
    No one—no one—what it knows.

PAN'S DEW-DROP.

PAN.

Hither, Sylphs and Satyrs, hither!
Here 's a secret going to wither:
Stand around and answer true,—
Is 't a gem or drop of dew?
Is its birthplace high or low,—
Sky or ocean? Ho—ho—ho!
    Ho—ho—ho!
Guess and tell me ere it go!

SYLPHS.

'Tis a tear from Luna's eye;
'Tis a star from some lost sky;
'Tis a fairy pearl—a thing
Fallen from Titania's ring!
'Tis a gem from Cupid's bow.

PAN.

Cupid! Cupid! Ho—ho—ho!
    Ho—ho—ho!
Cupid leaves no jewels so.

SYLPHS.

'Tis a spangle from the shoe
Which Queen Mab at Somnus threw;
'Tis a spark of Terra's spar!
Silver stud from Juno's car!
'Tis a rare and tiny shell
Gather'd from some Mermaid's cell!

PAN.

Mermaid! Juno! Ho—ho—ho!
    Ho—ho—ho!
'Tis but dew *that's frozen so.*

SYLPHS.

Who knows what it may conceal?
Atoms can great truths reveal!
Is 't a glowworm, fast asleep,
Caught and spell-bound ere 't could creep?
Is 't an egg some insect knew?

PAN.

Nothing else but frozen dew!
A bud! a berry! Guess who can:—
'Tis frozen dew, or I'm not Pan!

SYLPHS.

Winter ne'er such gem could show:
'Tis pearl!

PAN.

It is not! Ho—ho—ho!
Ho—ho—ho!
Here's a coil 'bout frost and snow!

THE MEADOW GATE.

The blue-bell peeps beneath the fern,
    The moor its purple blossom yields,
'Tis worth full six days' work to earn
    A ramble 'mid the woods and fields :
There is an hour to silence dear,
    An hour for which a king might wait;
It is to meet, when no one's near,
    My Mary by the meadow gate.

When love inspires the linnet's breast,
    How swift he speeds from spray to spray ;
His song is of his woodland nest,
    Far hidden from the peep of day.
Would such a nest were my sweet lot,
    Would I might be some dear one's mate ;
I'd ask, to share my lowly cot,
    My Mary by the meadow gate.

There is a tide the streamlet seeks,
    A full mile from its course it veers,
And into silvery music breaks
    When from the vale the sea appears.
Oh! twenty miles my eager feet
    Would wander long, and linger late,
One happy moment but to meet
    My Mary by the meadow gate.

BE SURE YOU CALL.

It was a rustic cottage gate,
    And over it a maiden leant,
Upon her face and youthful grace
    A lover's earnest eyes were bent.
" Good-night," she said, " once more, good-night,
    The evening star is rising high ;
But early with the morning light
    Be sure you call as you pass by.
        As you pass by,
    Be sure you call as you pass by."

The spring had into summer leapt,
    Brown autumn's hand her treasures threw,
When forth a merry party swept
    In bridal garments, two by two ;
I saw it was the maid that bless'd
    The evening star that rose so high :—

For he, as I suppose you 've guess'd,
  Had often call'd as he pass'd by,
    As he pass'd by,
  Had often call'd as he pass'd by.

Oh, blissful lot, where all 's forgot,
  Save love, that wreathes the heart with flowers!
Oh, what 's a throne to that dear cot
  Whose only wealth is happy hours?
And oft, if o'er the woodland way
  The evening star is rising high,
I fancy still I hear her say,
  " Be sure you call as you pass by,
    As you pass by,
  Be sure you call as you pass by."

FALSE AS WATER.

Flow on, thou faithless stream,
That maketh all things seem
   As deep within thy heart:
Fern, bell, and drooping tree,
Behold themselves in thee;
   And yet thou canst depart.
Alas! thy little span
But mimics faithless man!
   Like thee, too, he can stray:
Like thee a charm reveal—
Reflect, but never feel—
   And singing pass away.

Flow on! thou canst not touch
The wounded heart so much
   As man's inconstant breath:
Thy false tongue ne'er deceives
Like his, who loves, and leaves;
   Takes life, and brings us death!

What though within thy face
Our very looks we trace;
 Thy falsehood's not so deep
As his whose lips can sigh,
Yet leave the heart to die,—
 And, till it dies, to weep!

LOVERS' WALKS.

Ah! once I liked not lovers' walks,
    Nor wanderings by the hill,
When star to star at midnight talks,
    And all the world is still:
I laugh'd at all romantic souls,
    That half in rapture stood;
I hated strolls—those moonlight strolls—
    And always thought I should!

I vow'd by all the world e'er knew
    Of beautiful or bright,
No love on earth should tempt me to
    A rambling walk by night;
But, ah! one's mind can little guess
    To what one's heart is born!
Who'd thought a month, or even less,
    Had found me so forsworn?

But when I loved nor star, nor moon,
    Nor wanderings through the glen,
My song of life was out of tune,
    I knew not Mary then :
Now, I would rather roam till *light*
    Bloom'd o'er the Morn's sweet breast,
Than ever breathe those words, " Good Night! "
    Or ever think of rest.

THE DEVOTED.

I HEAR the organ's mellow peal
    Swelling the vast cathedral round;
But still a voice my soul doth feel
    Comes up between me and that sound.
I'm circled by a world that lives
    Within my heart, whose day or night
Is such as thy dear presence gives—
    If fled, 'tis dark—if near, 'tis light.
I know the bondage that detains,
    I feel that I'm no longer free;
Yet to my heart I clasp my chains,
    Content to be enthrall'd by thee!

I cannot think as I have thought;
    A power, 'tis fruitless to define,
Hath to my soul a vision brought—
    A presence—with a voice like thine!

It comes beside me unawares—
    It steps between me and the shrine ;
I clasp my hands to breathe my prayers,
    Yet say, " I'm thine, for ever thine ! "
Oh, where hath fled the tranquil rest,
    The freedom never more to be ?
Time seems but Sorrow in my breast,
    And life a void, till cheer'd by thee !

PLAIN FACES.

Neither feature nor complexion
    Can the law of liking prove;
We see all things through affection—
    All is lovely seen through love!

How we love, or what attraction
    Wins us, who hath power to learn!
Beauty, 'tis our satisfaction,
    Love can *this* in all discern!

Plainer faces win election,
    Plainer forms to passion move;
Joy, that through the heart's affection,
    Beauty lives in all we love!

NEVERMORE.

Whither, spirit, whither?
    Let me weep alone :
Wherefore bring me hither,
    Knowing she is gone?
All that was Elysian
    With herself hath flown ;
Tears are in the vision
    Of that shrine o'erthrown.

Do the roses whisper
    Sweet, as she were nigh?
Do the linnets warble
    Music, like her sigh?
Neither rose nor linnet
    Can the charm restore ;
Life hath but one language,
    One sad word—" Deplore ! "

Just as he that dreameth
 Starts, and wakes in tears,
So the present seemeth
 Girt with doubts and fears:
Still, 'mid hopes that wither,
 Sorrow liveth on:
Wherefore bring me hither,
 Knowing she is gone?

DID YOU KNOW HER?

Did you know her?—any station
    Might become her—high or low;
She was fond of admiration,
    Few the arts she did not know:
She could droop her eyes, as dreaming,
    With a tender, quiet grace;
Then, with sudden, upward beaming,
    Flash their lustre on your face!

Did you know her? She was never
    Fond of saying what she meant;—
You 'd confess her words were clever,
    But a riddle their intent:
She 'd a puzzle of expression,
    Half of nature, half of art;
And a perfect self-possession,
    Visible in every part.

Free and graceful in the morning,
    Pensive in the afternoon;
Changing moods without a warning—
    Weeping now—yet laughing soon:
Various as the moments show her,
    Still, each moment finds a charm;
And, indeed, if you should know her—
    Guard your heart—if it be warm!

NEVER FOUND.

There 's an image we enshrine
   In the heart's young days;
A form we deem divine
   In the heart's young days;
But that fancy of the mind,
We may seek—but never find:
'Tis a dream we leave behind
   With our heart's young days.

But who can dreams control
   In their heart's young days?
They 're the shadows of the soul,
   In our heart's young days:
And, though the *living* grace
May escape from our embrace,
Yet sweet 's the vision'd face
   Of our heart's young days!

'Tis the purity that waits
   On our heart's young days;
That such loveliness creates
   In our heart's young days:
The angel, that we drew,
Remain'd while life was new;
Then back to heaven flew
   With our heart's young days!

SMALL GIFTS.

I care not how simple
   The offering may be,
If it come from the heart
   It is welcome to me:
'Tis not in itself
   That the value resides;
The jewel is *love*—
   Worth all jewels besides.

Affection is something
   Beyond what is bought:
'Tis the growth of the heart—
   'Tis the wealth of the thought!
And often we find,
   'Mid the gifts of the earth,
The smallest in value
   Is greatest in worth!

LYRIC.

There's a spirit of fancy flowing—
　Flowing in dreams of night;
Sweeping the shores of darkness,
　Yet bearing an angel's light.

Restless—questioning ever—
　Reaping the fields of time,
Counting the unsown harvests,
　Longing the stars to climb.

What is the soul's true nature?
　What is the spirit's birth?
What is the mind's great sequel?
　Is it to end on earth?

Are we to love unceasing,
　There in that region of souls?
Sweetly the vision of heaven
　On to the Life-giver rolls!

That spirit of Fancy flowing,
 Flowing in dreams of night;
Sweeping the shores of darkness,
 Yet bearing an angel's light.

ROUND THE CORNER.

Round the corner waiting—
  What will people say?
If you wish to see me
  There's a proper way:
Village tongues are ever
  Ready with remark;
Eyes are at the casement
  If a dog but bark.
Round the corner waiting—
  What will people say?
If you wish to see me
  There's a proper way.

When the Church hath bound us,
  Link'd two hearts in one,
I shall care but little
  How their tongues rail on:

But until the bridal,
    Never let them find
Aught to cause me blushes—
    Hurt my peace of mind!
Round the corner waiting—
    What will people say?
Manly hearts should ever
    Take a manly way.

Fifty things are stated,
    Things you 'd ne'er suppose,
If but something secret
    In a neighbour shows:
Boldly take the pathway,
    And their lips are stayed;
All are quick to censure
    If you seem afraid.
Round the corner waiting—
    What will people say?
If you wish to see me
    There 's a proper way!

A WORD OF THINE.

A word of thine!—how hath it dwelt
   Like music in my heart!
A look!—how oft my soul hath knelt
   And worshipp'd it, apart!
My spirit like a mirror seems,
   That still, where'er I be,
In happy thoughts, or happier dreams,
   Reflects but only thee,
      My love,
   Reflects but only thee!

I marvel what my life had been
   If thee I ne'er had known?
Thy form, thy beauty, never seen,
   Nor heard thy lips' dear tone?

It seems as if my heart were born
    Thy shrine alone to be;
For every pulse from eve to morn
    Still beats for only thee,
        My love,
    Still beats for only thee!

THE BRITISH PRESS.

What 's nobler than the Press?
    Where else may Freedom find
The ready hand that can redress
    The wrongs of human kind?
It is a people's power—
    The terror of the strong:
Abler than armies in the hour
    Of tyranny and wrong.
The sword may strike oppression down;
    But sharper than the sword,
And mightier than a monarch's crown,
    The Press maintains its word!

It marks the footsteps of the age,
    The progress of the time;
Its seal is stamp'd on every page,
    In every land and clime:

It setteth principle above
    The brutal hand of force,
And forth, in usefulness and love,
    It runs its glorious course!
And they whose meaner minds can scheme
    To crush its honest sway,
As well, in fruitless hate, might dream
    To check the light of day.

What 's dearer than the Press
    To every manly heart?
What voice is first the right to bless,
    To act the patriot's part?
The spirit, manners, customs, arts,
    Opinions, changes,—all
That worth to human life imparts,—
    Its columns can recall.
It moves—and every bar is hurl'd
    Athwart its path like weeds!
It speaks—and it divides the world
    In parties, powers, and creeds!

The textures of our social state,
    The aspects of the past,—
When different creeds fed mutual hate,
    And conscience overcast,—

These live within its potent lines,
    And ancient errors show;
From *these* a guiding spirit shines
    Which every man should know.
When stood the Press with front of steel,
    While meaner champions fled?
When it was crime to set the heel
    Upon the serpent's head!

What's holier than the Press,
    Which hallows every home;
Which lifts the darkness from distress,
    And points the light to come!
Which teaches faith when hope is dull;
    And, onward as we plod,
Reveals to us the beautiful,
    Uprising like a god!
For not uncared for, in his day
    Of sorrow, man hath been:
Angels have watched his troubled way,
    And helped him when unseen!

'Tis true the men are few
    That turn with grateful hearts,
To names where every meed is due
    That human fame imparts:

'Tis easy to forget
    The patriot debt we owe;
But there are dates in history yet
    Time cannot overthrow!
The men that battled for the right
    When right was hard to win;
Who braved the axe, and laugh'd at might,
    When Might called *Freedom* sin.

Great hearts have girt thee round,
    O Press, revered of yore!
Burke, Milton, More, have crown'd
    Thy rule for evermore!
Their sacred banner was "Advance!"
    Integrity their guide,
And Truth the consecrated lance
    That swept each bar aside!
Such are the names our land should bless!
    The song of age and youth
Should still be, Honour to the Press,
    And Victory to Truth!

Then, if thy power be great,
    Great be thy justice too;
Be fearless in thy place to state
    Whate'er to man is due.

Be thou to every heart a guide,
    A lamp to every mind;
So shall thy course be sanctified—
    Teaching, as GOD design'd;
And never be thy power abused,
    Thy mission here misled;
Oh, never may thou stand accused
    Before the Patriot Dead!

Lend Education aid
    Where'er thy voice can reach;
No text is more obey'd
    Than that the Press can preach.
Bid trade the wide earth span;
    Speed labour to its due;
Bid mind-enlightened man
    GOD's Eden-world renew.
Still every good befriend,
    And every ill enthral,
Till man's improvement end
    But with the end of all!

BIRTHDAY LYRIC.

Down the ladder of Aurora,
When she hath the day before her,
   And the East is clasp'd in gold,
Saw I angels swift descending,
With a glory never-ending,
   And a majesty untold;
And I whisper'd lowly—slowly—
" Whither tend ye, angels holy?"
Spake they forth—" We bring affection
To a heart of our selection—
To the birthday of a being
We, afar from heaven seeing,
Loved: and bear, by Faith's direction,
One pure, priceless gift—Affection!"

Then the scene, like music, fainted
   Far away in waves of light;
And a vision like one sainted,
In some old cathedral painted,
   Flash'd its wonder on my sight!

BIRTHDAY LYRIC.

Down a silvery pathway gliding,
In a robe of starry binding,
  Moved the Presence upon earth ;
And I sought my fear to banish,
Lest, in speaking, it might vanish,
  Saying, " Whither, angel fair ? "
  And it whisper'd, soft as air,
" I bring gifts to one, whose spirit
Well deserveth to inherit—
Friendship, *that departeth never !*
Love, still faithful, fond for ever !
Equal to a life's endurance—
To another world's securance !
So, when death to heaven may guide her,
Love shall linger still beside her,
Friendship mourn o'er days departed,
Nature weep for the true-hearted ;
Virtue every gift commendeth,
May she keep them till life endeth ! "

Fled my dream ;—for Morn, the singer,
  O'er my couch her sunbeams held ;
And with touch of golden finger
  All my angel-world dispell'd !
Ah, methought, if love were given
  Thus, how we should prize its worth—

In its nature all of heaven
    That might enter aught of earth!
Ah, if friendship falter'd never,
Heart to heart, and thus for ever!

Yet ourselves *within* must find
Charm to gain, and skill to bind;
Soul must shine ere friendship's won—
There's no summer without sun!
Heart must glow ere love can rest,
And call GOD's angel to the breast!

CHRIST BLESSING LITTLE CHILDREN.

If there were language in each star,
    A voice in every onward wave;
If every breeze that travell'd far,
    An ever-during utterance gave;
They yet must fail to tell the worth
Of those blest words Christ spake on earth.

Oh morn, it was no light of sun
    That left such glory on thy face!
It was a light in Christ begun—
    A sun that ne'er will run its race!
A light—a sun—whose endless ray
Shall cheer affliction's darkest day!

Blest words, that wider circle fill
    Than frail humanity can span:
That thrill—and shall for ages thrill—
    The universal heart of man:
Words with eternal comfort rife—
Words throbbing with immortal life!

Though weak the little feet that came
    Half coyly to the SAVIOUR's side;
Though small the lips that lisp'd His name,
    Though check'd by His disciples' pride,
He, who beholdeth all things, saw
In each child's face GOD's written law.

As in the seed we know the flower
    That future suns shall wake to birth;
So, in the child, CHRIST saw that *dower*
    Which speaks of other worlds than earth!
That germ which sleeps in quiet might
Till GOD shall call it into light!

Though *they* could neither see nor hear
    What then our SAVIOUR saw and heard—
The glory of another sphere!
    The music of JEHOVAH's word!
To *His* divine humanity
All things of heaven were open'd free.

Oh, fitting theme for painter's art,
    That brings the Past before man's eyes;
That bids him from no portion part,
    Till angels meet him in the skies!
What worthier theme for painter's skill
Than *hope* which Christian truths fulfil?

He, who did little children bless,
  Will still receive and bless them now :
Kneel to Him in your loveliness—
  Pray for His hand to press your brow :
That hand which life to all hath given,
That welcomes all from earth to heaven !

Christ waiteth !—shall your Saviour plead,
  And you, with children at your knee,
Still pause, their little steps to lead,
  To Him who loves them *more than ye ?*
Teach, father, teach the way He trod ;
Lead, mother, lead thy child to God !

IMPLORA PACEM.

Lowly, lowly, lying lowly,
    Where the willow weeps,
One who makes remembrance holy
    In her beauty sleeps.
Music once was in the river,
    Joy in wood and field,
Gone are they, and gone for ever,
    Earth no charm can yield.

Like a star the cloud o'ershadeth,
    Did we lose her ray;
Like a flower that blooms and fadeth,
    Faded she away;
None remember, none come hither
    Mourning o'er her doom—
None, save one, whose heart is with her,
    In her village tomb.

IMPLORA PACEM.

Wild birds seek the willow near her,
    Singing as of yore;
She whose voice was sweeter, dearer,
    Sings to me no more.
Every charm was thrown about her
    That could life adorn;
Now the sun is dark without her
    And the world forlorn.

Something blest to her was given,
    Some diviner birth;
There's one angel more in heaven,
    And one miss'd from earth.
Every hope my heart refuseth
    Thinking but of *one!*
Ah, we know not what life loseth
    'Till the loved are gone!

LINES

WRITTEN ON THE DEATH OF MISS FLEMING.

INSCRIBED TO WILLIAM FLEMING, ESQ., M.D.

———◆———

There's a land where hearts united
    Live, unknowing change or time;
Where the leaves and flowers unblighted
    Speak of an eternal clime:
There's a land that knows not sorrow,
    Sees not tears of anguish flow;
Fears no trial for the morrow—
    To that land, oh, let us go!

Here affection still is weeping
    Over friends that must depart;
Here we love—but there's no keeping
    Those we love around our heart.
Where's the home that death bereaves not?
    Where's the heart that ne'er felt woe?
To that land where friendship grieves not—
    To that land, oh, let us go!

LINES ON THE DEATH OF MISS FLEMING.

From the morn a ray is darting,
    Which must end in clouds of night;
On the earth we read but " Parting!"
    Leaf and flower the same word write.
To that land where Morning dies not,
    Where the skies immortal glow,
Where the heart in parting sighs not—
    To that land, oh, let us go!

There—where angels are repeating
    Hymns to God, who doth restore
Heart to heart in endless meeting—
    Boundless love for evermore.
Mother, 'tis a child that names thee,
    'Tis a seraph whispers low;
Brother, 'tis a sister claims thee—
    To that land, oh, let us go!

In affliction's hour of trial,
    Let our faith more perfect rise;
Teach our love a brief denial,
    Ask that peace which God supplies!
So the future shall grow dearer,
    Knowing what it can bestow:
So our mission shall be clearer
    In that land to which we go!

HELP EACH OTHER.

I never knew a kindness yet,
  But, as Time's seasons ran,
Some seed of hope from it was set
  That promised good for man :
I never knew a feeling heart,
  In needful cases shown,
But it a spirit could impart
  Congenial to its own !

For kindness is a power divine,
  An essence not of earth ;
It wreathes the everlasting shrine
  Where holiest things have birth :
It hath a life beyond to-day ;
  And, when this life is o'er,
'Twill meet us smiling on our way,
  And good for good restore !

I never knew a generous hand
　　Grow poorer for such deed ;
A power we all can understand
　　Still bids that hand succeed.
Whate'er a noble act may cost,
　　Whate'er the service given,
A kindness done is never lost ;
　　Neither on earth nor heaven!

A DAY AGO.

A DAY!—a thing but few regard—
   A drop upon the stream of life—
A flower upon the summer sward,
   Where thousand other flowers are rife!
Yet o'er the dial of our fate
   There is a finger moving slow;
How long 't will move, what tongue can state?
   What's death was *life* a day ago!

Ah! solemn task, to teach the soul
   The value of a moment's space;
Our thoughts and wishes to control,
   And look on Truth with fearless face!
To strip from Hope its rainbow dress,
   Its false, false glitter, and its show:
All life—to man—is littleness!
   All time—to GOD—a day ago!

Use time, and use it wisely, then;
   Esteem it at its proper worth;
Nor say, were years to come again,
   We would act differently on earth.
Be grateful for the bounties sent,
   And patient when they cease to flow;
Soon—soon—we learn how much is meant
   By those brief words—A day ago!

GOOD ADVICE.

Who receives advice with kindness—
   Marks its simple, plain intent?
Who, discarding selfish blindness,
   Taketh counsel as 'tis meant?
Ah! too often, what was merely
   Urged to caution or improve,
Toucheth vanity too nearly,
   Hurts our feeling—pride—self-love

Surely, hearts of wiser feeling,
   Should be joyed to find a friend
Any hint or thought revealing,
   Formed to warn, instruct, amend.
Courtly phrase and false pretences,
   Outward smile and servile show,
May indeed avoid offences:
   Friends a higher office know!

What, though other lips may pander
   To each weakness of our youth,
Better to receive with candour,
   Honest, open, manly truth.
Take, then, truth without resistance,
   Use it, and its worth discern ;
To the last day of existence
   All have something yet to learn.

THE MERRY HEART.

'Tis well to have a merry heart,
    However short we stay:
There's wisdom in a merry heart,
    Whate'er the world may say.
Philosophy may lift its head
    And find out many a flaw,
But give me the philosophy
    That's happy with a straw.

If life but bring us happiness,
    It brings us, we are told,
What's hard to buy, though rich ones try
    With all their heaps of gold.
Then laugh away, let others say
    Whate'er they will of mirth;
Who laughs the most may truly boast
    He's got the wealth of earth.

THE MERRY HEART.

There 's beauty in a merry laugh,
    A moral beauty, too :
It shows the heart 's an honest heart,
    That 's paid each man his due ;
And lent a share of what 's to spare,
    Despite of wisdom's fears,
And made the cheek less sorrow speak,
    The eye weep fewer tears.

The sun may shroud itself in cloud,
    The tempest-wrath begin ;
It finds a spark to cheer the dark,
    Its sunlight is within.
Then laugh away, let others say
    Whate'er they will of mirth ;
Who laughs the most may truly boast
    He 's got the wealth of earth.

THE MAGIC GLASS.

Hither maidens, merry maidens!
    Come and view my magic glass!
I can tell you many marvels,
    All things as they 're sure to pass!
I can see adventure growing,
    Through a mystic power sublime;
Watch the hand of Fortune throwing
    Treasures in the lap of Time!
Come then, maidens, merry maidens!
    Come and see my magic glass!
All the wonders I shall whisper,
    True as time, are sure to pass!

Time, that like a seed appeareth,
    Dry and dark, and hard to view:
I can show you how it reareth
    Leaf, and bud, and flow'ret too:

Leaf of friendship, coyly hidden,
    Flower of love, that shuns the sight!
Things to other eyes forbidden,
    Unto mine are clear as light!
Come then, maidens, merry maidens!
    Come and view my magic glass!
All the wonders I shall whisper,
    True as time, are sure to pass!

Like a stage I see the future,—
    Signs and symbols o'er it crowd,
Wild as wintry stars at midnight,
    And they speak to me aloud:
Tell me secrets worth believing,
    Secrets with instruction rife—
What the loom of Fate is weaving
    From the mingled threads of life.
Come then, maidens, merry maidens!
    Come and view my magic glass!
All the wonders I shall whisper,
    Sure as time, shall come to pass!

PAST AND PRESENT.

With the solitude of ages,
　In the hoary woods sublime,
Hung two vast and glorious cages,
　Which belong'd to Time.
Songs from one came, sweet and pleasant,
　From the other hope seem'd cast—
The merry bird was called the Present,
　The melancholy bird the Past.

Time, I saw, was feeding ever
　His sweet favourite from his store;
But the Past he came to never,
　Though she 'd been his joy before!
Still the Past would give its warning,
　"Not so long wilt thou be dear!"
Though the bird sang night and morning,
　Never would the Present hear!

THE FORTRESS.

What fortress spans this rock forlorn?
    What sea mourns at its feet?
Its walls " might laugh a siege to scorn,"
    Its tide engulph a fleet!

Yet rusted swing its iron gates;
    Scant guard the warder keeps;
One at the portal stands and waits,—
    One stands, and waits, and weeps.

The banner lifts its batter'd crest
    Above the shipless tide;
The harbour seems in little quest,
    Nor pilot here, nor guide.

Ho! tell me who this fortress claims?
    Who claims? the watcher saith—
One who with joy each angel names,
    The heir of all is Faith!

And 'tis the banner of our GOD
 That floats upon the morn;
This is the Rock that all have trod
 Who 've sprung, through Faith, new born.

Though few the feet that enter in,
 Yet shall a day appear,
When GOD shall strike the gates of sin,
 And all shall enter here.

LINES

ON THE DEATH OF SIR JOHN POTTER, M.P., FOUNDER OF THE FREE LIBRARY.

Life and Death—two words containing
   More than human thought can span :
What is Death?—the dust remaining
   Utters no response to man.

We behold :—but earthly vision
   Cannot compass that domain,
Cannot climb that world Elysian
   Where the dead new life attain.

Life is *duty!*—noblest therefore
   He who best that course selects ;
Never waiting, asking " Wherefore ?"—
   Acting as his heart directs !

Feeling, that through Education
   Lies the secret of all good ;
That to make a happy nation,
   Men must first be understood !

Know each other—aid each other—
    Short the space 'twixt life and death,
When the lowest shall be brother
    To the highest that have breath.

Thou who felt for human labour,
    Knew its means and pleasures few,
Thou that sought thy humbler neighbour;
    Teaching *others* what to do!

Thousands,—in the far to-morrow,—
    Shall survey this hallowed ground,
And with tears of silent sorrow
    Bless the friend their fathers found!

All that is of power or beauty
    Passeth from our steps away;
In the path of *Faith* and *Duty*
    Honour lives, though Man decay.

OLD FRIENDS AND OLD TIMES.

Thinking of old times,
  Hopes ne'er to be;
Speaking of old friends
  Far o'er the sea:
Distance can change not
  Dear ones like you;
Fortune estrange not
  Hearts that are true!
Thus, in the twilight,
  Fond thoughts will stray
Back to the old homes—
  Homes far away!

Oh! 'mid the old friends,
  I no more see,
Is there a kind thought
  Ever for me?

If there 's but *one* hope,
   One wish, though vain ;
If there 's but *one* sigh,
   I 'll not complain.
Thus in the twilight
   Tears oft will stray,
Thinking of old friends,—
   Friends far away.

WHAT IS THAT WE TAKE FROM EARTH?

What is that we take from earth
    When the spirit leaves its clay?
What is there of mortal birth
    Worthy to be borne away?
Is it state, or power, or fame,
    Gold or rank, we need above?
Oh! there's nought worth heaven's claim
    Save that gift of heaven—*love!*
Love, which fills the world with light,
    When the sun hath set afar,
Love, which joins us in our flight
    To that land where angels are!

From all nature doth it draw
    Beauty to adorn its shrine;
By some spiritual law
    Making earthly things divine.

It the inner soul inspires,
    It the purer life reveals ;
And eternity requires
    To express the faith it feels !
Love, 'tis Love, fills earth with light,
    When the sun hath set afar ;
Love, which joins us in our flight
    To that world where angels are !

Yes, 'mid all that GOD hath made
    There is one surpassing spell ;
In its strength are saints array'd,
    In its glory angels dwell.
It is this which still outspeeds
    Sight and space, and time and breath,
It is this the spirit needs
    When immortal over death !
Sweetness which outblooms the May,
    Brightness which outshines the star ;
This, 'tis this, we bear away
    To that land where angels are !

TO THE YOUNG.

If a dower to man were granted,
  Free and boundless in extent,
Hills on which renown was planted,
  Soil for widest culture meant;
What would be the donor's sorrow
  If that unattended earth
Show'd no promise for the morrow,
  Nothing but defect and dearth?

Or, if some small cultivation,
  But in patches scatter'd o'er,
Flowers—a few for decoration—
  Just in front, and nothing more!
All the vast extent behind it
  Left without one seed to grow;
Left—as Time ought ne'er to find it,
  Since God bade the sun to glow!

TO THE YOUNG.

Oh, the gift of mind is greater
    Than the gift of land can be :
Nothing from our kind Creator
    Breathes so much of deity :
Nothing through the world's extension
    Equals that eternal dower ;
Scarce an angel's comprehension
    Spans the vastness of its power!

If, then, but a *thin partition*
    Of that mind true culture knows,
If no tillage gains admission,
    Nought that right advancement shows,
Is it grateful to the Donor
    Who—some purpose to fulfil—
Made ye of such power the owner,
    To be careless of his will?

Is it grateful to the spirit
    Poorly thus its worth to scan,
To neglect what you inherit,
    Disregard God's gift to man ?
Is it wise to rest contented
    With this half-instructed state ?
Lost time ne'er was unrepented,
    But regret may come too late!

Work then, youth, while yet 'tis morning,
  Broad the land before you lies,
Neither task nor labour scorning;
  Which the fruit of thought supplies;
As you work so choose your station,
  Knowing life and its demands;
Knowing 'tis through cultivation
  That the living mind expands!

A HEART FOR EVERY ONE.

Oh! there's a heart for every one,
    If every one could find it;
Then up and seek, ere youth be gone,
    Whate'er the toil ne'er mind it!
For if you chance to meet at last
    With that *one* heart, intended
To be a blessing unsurpass'd,
    Till life itself is ended,
How would you prize the labour done,
    How grieve if you 'd resign'd it;
For there's a heart for every one,
    If every one could find it.

Two hearts are made, the angels say,
    To suit each other dearly;
But each one takes a different way,
    A way not found so clearly!—

Yet though you seek, and seek for years,
    The trouble's worth the taking,
For what the life of home endears
    Like hearts of angels' making?
Then haste, and guard the treasure won,
    When fondly you've enshrin'd it;
For there's a heart for every one,
    If every one could find it?

MAIDENHOOD.

My love is full of happy mirth,
    Her laughter is a joy to see;
And yet there's scarce a thing on earth
    She wishes not to be!

A flower, in some green covert found,
    Half hidden from the view:
"Ah! well," I said, "were I the ground
    On which thy beauty grew!"

A bird, that sky-ward might repair,
    Or soar to heavenly things:
"Yes, were I but the blessed air
    That bore thy glittering wings!"

Then she would like a river be,
    With green banks sweeping wide;
And I—I'd be some willow tree
    Still whispering by her side.

" Can I be nothing without *you?* "
　　She poutingly replied :
All things, to one another true,
　　I said, must be allied ?

As well divorce the air from light,
　　The colour from the flower,
As banish me from that dear sight
　　In which I live each hour !

" If such a lot must me befal,—
　　Though bird, or flower, or star,
I think," she smiled, " that after all,
　　We 're better as we are ! "

THANK GOD FOR ALL.

Beside yon oak a rustic roof appears,
  A cottage garden leads unto the door,
A few wild plants the lowly casement cheers,
  And all around looks neat, though all is poor.
There Philip dwells, and takes a neighbour's part,
  Though little be the means his help to test;
Yet still, though poor, he says, with grateful heart,
  'Tis well to labour,—and that God knows best!

The hare flits by him with her dewy feet,
  As blithe of heart he quits his cottage gate:
The golden village lane with dawn is sweet,
  And Philip feels content, though low his state;
For labour unto him can joy impart,
  'Tis independence to his honest breast;
And still, though poor, he says, with grateful heart,
  'Tis well to labour,—and that God knows best!

His wife beside the door waits his return,
    His children's voices meet him half the way,
And while the sun within the west doth burn,
    And bird and brook sing sweet the close of day,
Philip forgets his toil, his chair to find,
    By little arms and little lips caress'd;
And gazing round, exclaims, with grateful mind,
    Thank God for all,—thank God, who knoweth best!

THE CROSS OF CHRIST.

INSCRIBED TO THE REV. J. M. BELLEW, S.C.L.

———•———

O CROSS of CHRIST! first rear'd 'mid scoff and scorn,
    Cherish'd in secret 'gainst a bad world's hate:
Now on the neck of maiden beauty worn—
    Blazing 'mid arms and banners of the state—
The flags of navies, crown'd and consecrate!
    Erst type of persecution, shame, and blood;
Now the bow'd knees of nations on thee wait;
    And kings adore, where burning martyrs stood,
Like Faith amidst the flames, unchanged and un-
    subdued!

O blest of Heaven, Religion, GOD-born guide!
    Not thine the torture and the bigot chain,
Not thine the unsparing creed, the zealot pride
    That would, through persecution, CHRIST attain!

Thou hast no heavenly joy in human pain;
  But ever com'st by love and mercy led;
Yet wert thou *parent* call'd by many a Cain,
  Who from the altar struck his brother dead,
And pray'd with gore-stain'd hands, as if 'twere incense
    shed!

Come to our souls and make us all thine own;
  Come with thy brow of truth, thy lip of grace—
Thy peace, which is the light of JESUS' throne;
  Thy hope, which beameth like an angel's face;
Oh, come, Religion, all the world embrace!
  For all are brothers, and GOD's home would seek:
Back to thy breast our erring footsteps trace;
  Teach us with Christian charity to speak,
Nor crouch to high estate, nor trample on the weak!

To preach the Gospel!—to illume the dark,
  Strengthen the weak, upraise the poor and low;
To seek in humble breasts the struggling spark,
  And with the breath of truth to bid it glow:
To lead the frail, irresolute, and slow
  Unto the fount of everlasting light!
To teach them to believe what GOD doth show
  In every dawning day and setting night:
To call the erring back, and guide their feet aright.

This is to preach the Gospel of our Lord!
  To lead through love, persuade through Mercy's
    tongue:
And thou, to whom I dedicate each word,
  Whose zeal, whose genius I have honour'd long,
Still, arm'd with eloquence, convince the throng;
  Assure the doubtful—win the heedless breast,
Bid lips, long mute, thrill with JEHOVAH's song!
  Show the afflicted where their griefs may rest,—
So shall thy name be loved, and thy true mission blest!

THE OLD EVENINGS.

I WANDER'D by the old house,
   But others now live there;
I thought about the old times
   And all we used to share.
How happy 'twas our wont to meet,
   When friends came frank and free.
Ah, when shall we such faces greet
   As once we used to see
In those old merry evenings,
Those pleasant friendly evenings,
   Beneath the old roof tree?

But what though we'd the old house,
   We still should lack old cheer,
The old friends in the old house
   Were all that made it dear!

And these are fled, or changed, or dead,
   And never more may we
Revive the music of their tread—
   The joys that used to be
In those old friendly evenings,
Those long-departed evenings,
   Beneath the old roof tree!

THE CHARITIES OF LIFE.

If thou hast pass'd an aching heart.
   Turn back a little way,
Let not "*thy giving*" be a part
   To act another day !
Give whilst the weary eye is dim,
   And if a tear should fall,
'Twill be in gratitude to Him
   Who heard the mourner's call.
Oh, in the charities of life
   This impulse still obey ;
And if thou 'st *pass'd* an aching heart
   Turn back a little way !

It is not far the feet can go ;
   The shadow cometh fast ;
And whether we move fast or slow,
   'Tis to one bourn at last.

When thy " to-morrows " all have died,
    Kind actions will appear
Like angels waiting at thy side
    To bless thee, and to cheer!
Then in the charities of life
    This impulse still obey;
And if thou 'st *pass'd* an aching heart
    Turn back a little way!

LITTLE REQUIRED.

'Tis little indeed we require,
   A cot just removed from the way,
All cover'd with woodbine and briar,
   And Norah still with me each day.
We can live upon nothing at all,
   For what do we care for display?
Love can smile though his income be small,
     Yes, that's what he used to say!
     Ah, me! that's what he used to say!

Then love before marriage could see
   No figure so fair as my own;
Now figures in columns of three
   Perplex him and alter his tone!
He wonders how bills can come in
   In this strange unaccountable way:
And frowns, with his hand to his chin,
     And forgets what he used to say,
     Ah, me! forgets what he used to say!

He says that he loves me the same,—
    There's nothing, at least, I detect;—
But a maid when she changes her name
    Hath many a change to expect.
I wish better times would appear,
    That Harry again might be gay,
And whisper once more in my ear
    The words that he used to say,
    Ah, me! the words that he used to say!

EVERYBODY'S GIPSY.

Hope 's the Gipsy queen of life,
   Fortune's hidden light revealing;
Whisp'ring better stars are rife
   In the depths the cloud 's concealing:
She is seen at many gates—
   Many sighs to her are given;—
If we credit all she states,
   She 's her knowledge straight from heaven.
More than any gipsy known
   She sets all things in confusion:
She 's the one whose power alone
   Keeps the whole world in delusion!

Kings and peers her voice obey,
   High and low her spells she tosses:
E'en the poor and aged stay
   When their path of life she crosses:

Soldiers on the tented field,
    Sailors on the stormy ocean,
Unto her their secrets yield;
    None on earth have such devotion.
More than any gipsy known
    She sets all things in confusion;
She's the one whose power alone
    Keeps the whole world in delusion.

WHAT'S YOUR OPINION?

'Tis my belief, that if you show
Your heart to any one you know,
Or let your cheek with blushes glow,
    You shorten Love's dominion:
But if you pause, or seem to be
Indifferent to his urgent plea;
The colder you—the warmer he:
    Now tell me your opinion,
        Your opinion;
    Do tell me your opinion.

'Tis hard when feelings' pulse beats strong
To guard the word that seeks the tongue;
And hide the secret well—and long:
    But who would *lose* dominion?

Who let a little word defeat
The hopes that in their bosoms beat?
Whate'er I felt—he should not see 't!
 At least, that 's my opinion,
  My opinion;
 At least, that 's my opinion!

'Tis said that some are far too nice,
Too over-proud to take advice;
I only pray you to think twice
 Before you quit dominion:
The more your looks, your lips, express.
The more you sigh, he 'll sigh the less;
'Till he *proposed* I 'd ne'er *confess!*
 At least, that 's my opinion,
  My opinion;
 At least, that 's *my* opinion!

THE WHEREWITHAL.

A MAN may have wisdom and worth.
   And humour and wit at his call;
But what do these matter on earth
   If he has not the wherewithal?
His home may be circled with friends,
   If he only can keep up the ball;
But friendship soon changes and ends
   If he has not the wherewithal.
Then seek for the wherewithal—
   Make sure of the wherewithal,
For pleasure, like friendship, soon ends
   If you have not the wherewithal.

The *purse* is the dial whose face
   Shows best where the sunlight doth fall;
He always is first in the race,
   Who is first with the wherewithal!

THE WHEREWITHAL.

Some say that the high can be mean—
    Some hint that the great can be small;
But trifles like these are not seen,
    If bless'd with the wherewithal!
Then seek for the wherewithal—
    Make sure of the wherewithal,
For pleasure, like friendship, soon ends,
    If short of the wherewithal.

Love smiles on the casement that shows
    A picture *within* to enthral;
When *gold* 's in the heart of the rose,
    There 's *love* in the wherewithal?
Yes; men may have wisdom and worth,
    And humour and wit at their call,
But what do these matter on earth
    If they have not the wherewithal!
Then seek for the wherewithal—
    Make sure of the wherewithal,
For pleasure, like friendship, soon ends,
    If short of the wherewithal!

PASSING AWAY.

I.

Look from the casement!—look, and tell
    What's passing, mother, dear;
Since dawn I've heard a funeral bell,
    Slow pealing on my ear;
And now there comes the solemn fall
    Of footsteps sweeping nigh.
Look down the street, I hear their feet,
    Some funeral's passing by.
The mother gazed with anxious face,
    But nothing there was seen,
Except each old accustom'd place,
    And what had always been.

II.

A moment yet, dear mother, stay:
    Strange sounds are on the air,
Like angels singing on their way
    Or voices deep in prayer!

Oh, lift my pillow high—more high—
    For I am faint and low ;
Help me to look upon the sky,
    And bless them ere they go !
The mother raised her daughter's head,
    But no word could she speak ;
The hope that from her bosom sped
    Left tears upon her cheek.

III.

The night look'd through the casement old,
    And saw a cheek so pale—
A form so wasted, thin, and cold—
    No skill might there prevail ;
But that which conquers Death yet beam'd
    Upon her wasted brow ;
And sweet, as though an angel dream'd,
    The sufferer rested now !
Ah, who the mother's grief may tell ?
    Or who may comfort bring ?
Yet, high above the funeral bell,
    She heard the angels sing !

DEAD, YET UNDIVIDED.

They are together still,—
　The parted still are one!
Their *love* our being's home can fill,
　Although the loved be gone!
The mystery of the spirit's birth
　Outfathoms human skill;
Though one's in heaven, and one on earth,
　They are together still!

For there's a feeling that unites
　The distant and the dead;
The last sweet bloom that winter blights,
　Yet leaves the odour shed:
And thus affection lives beyond
　Death's dark and withering will;
No power hath he to part the fond,—
　They meet, in spirit, still!

In quiet thought, in lonely prayer,
    That spirit all pervades,
It lends a glory to the air
    When every planet fades;
It circles all with holiness,
    It blunts the barb of ill;
And e'en the parted it can bless,
    And link together still!

THE HOPES GONE BY.

The hopes gone by—the hopes that made
   A golden path to other years ;
Ere yet our hearts had known a shade,
   Or life had lost what life endears :
The bounding heart—the spirits' play—
   The thoughts that seem'd on wings to fly—
We ask in vain,—ah, where are they?
   The days, the dreams, the hopes gone by !

The brightness and the bloom have fled,
   And life seems cold as wintry snow ;
For some are changed, and some are dead,
   That knew and loved us long ago !
Those golden visions come no more
   As once they came, when hope was high,
Yet dear, till life's last pulse is o'er,
   Will be the days, the hopes, gone by !

FLOWERS.

Flowers, sweet Flora's children!
  How ye sport and spring,
Smiling between bank and brook,
Mossy marge, and woody nook,
  Where the linnets sing;
Climbing hedgerow, bush, and brier,
As your spirit ne'er would tire,
  Thorough lane and lea:
Full of life, and full of mirth,
Ye alone enjoy the earth,—
  Happy children ye!

Flowers, sweet Flora's children!
  How ye roam and race,
By the valley—up the hill,
With an everchanging will,
  Haunting every place;

FLOWERS.

Hanging half-way down the steep,
Where the wild stag dare not leap,
   In your reckless glee;
Or, where snows eternal blanch,
Listening to the avalanche,—
   Bold adventurers ye!

Flowers, sweet Flora's children!
   How ye dance and twine
With the loveliest born of Spring,
Moving in an endless ring—
   An exhaustless line!
Sometimes shy and singly seen,
Like some nun, in cloister green,
   Offering incense free;
Sometimes over marsh and moor,
Resting by the cottage-door,—
   Welcome comers ye!

Flowers, dear Flora's children!
   How ye love to meet
Far away from human sound,
Making Nature hallow'd ground—
   Even loneness sweet;
Where some fount, 'mid mountain-springs,
Singing falls, and falling sings

In melodious key;
Blooming where no step is heard,
Save the light foot of some bird,—
  Favour'd children ye!

Flowers, sweet Flora's children!
  Loved by moon and star;
Loved by little ramblers lone,
Seated on some grassy stone,—
  Many a footstep far!
Loved by all that God hath made,
All that ever watch'd and pray'd:
  For ye seem to me,
In your bright and boundless span,
Silent speakers unto man
  Of the world to be!

SYMPATHY.

As chords in unison respond,
    So feel our minds a like control.
A fine and spiritual bond,
    A sympathy of soul with soul!
Where feelings, like the stars divine,
    That o'er the waters' troubled way,
So meet and mingle as they shine
    That God alone could part each ray!

And thus with those, by heaven design'd,
    A mental brotherhood to know,
That fine affinity of mind
    Where genial thoughts commingling glow:
Where, oh, so tuned the being's chords,
    So sweetly like each waken'd tone,
We hear—we think—our very words!
    And every feeling seems our own!

Or, like the earth which flowerless pines,
   Still mute and cold to alien hours,
When once a kindred sunbeam shines,
   Like magic shows its thousand flowers!
Thus myriad hues of mind and heart
   Lie hid from spirits unallied;
But let a kindred soul-ray start,
   And beauty blooms on every side!

MORN.

See morn o'er the heavens
    Is sailing divine;
Her barque is all golden
    And purple each line;
Her flag blue and crimson;
    And over the skies
She sweeps in her beauty,
    To gladden all eyes.

The chequer'd horizon
    Spreads wide on the sight,
Like islands of glory
    Where angels alight!
And the barque dashes onward
    O'er billows of clouds,
Whilst the lark, like a sailor,
    Sings high 'mid the shrouds!

Oh! that man through life's voyage,
　　Whatever storm wars,
Would keep his soul's pennant
　　Still fix'd 'mid the stars!
Till the harbour appearing,
　　For which he had striven,
Life's vessel might rest,
　　Safely anchor'd in Heaven.

THE HIDDEN DELL.

O'er a wide heath whose purple bloom had fled,
Or fallen low for winds to sweep about,
Just as Aurora show'd her drowsy head,
As if to wake or slumber still in doubt,
    Straight from the path—the rude, broad path, scoop'd out
Abrupt and startling—there appear'd a dell,
From whose green mouth, as from some shrine devout,
The panting waters seem'd with pride to swell,
Then down the rocky cleft with rapid music fell.

By root, or rock, or hanging bush I sped,
Until a broken arch and gate were seen,
That to a strange deserted garden led;
O'ergrown, and all one melancholy green,
Save here and there some flowery shrub between,
Or ancient statue from its column cast,—
    A majesty of grandeur that had been
    A memory of the proud and prosperous past,—
Stood haughty in decay—still stately to the last!

With sighs the woods unto my step replied,
And from the trembling leaves hung many a tear,
Which the stern winds, as angry, brush'd aside—
For what might tears avail gaunt ruin here?
Nor grief could change, nor gleam of gladness cheer
The desolation and the blight around:
Yet one lone flower, like infant beauty near,
Kiss'd with its honey'd lip the wither'd ground,
And smiled upon the thorns to which its bloom was
bound.

Something, I know not what, detain'd me there:
'Midst grandeur and neglect I wander'd on,
Till, all at once, the path show'd touch of care;
In golden groups the tended flowrets shone,
Bright as Love's footsteps, and as swiftly gone;
A broken rose-stem, with a ribbon tied,
Told of a maiden's hand—some lovely one
Perchance still near: quick sought I every side,
But still nor fluttering veil, nor vestment white espied.

Anon the pathway turn'd—a steep ascent—
Then lost itself in venerable shade;
My very breath with toil seem'd almost spent,
When shot a gleam of silver through the glade.

Some bird its home and happy nest had made
By path which human footstep rarely chose ;
Willing to seek, and yet to stir afraid,
Tiptoe I followed where the dim boughs close,
And looking down beheld my Maiden of the Rose.

Half hid 'mid waves and weeds the maiden stood,
Bathing her beauty in the happy brook,
Whose waters clasp'd her in a pearly flood ;
Or, flowing fondly, stole an upward look,
As of her beauty they some portion took ;
Then, turning, leapt unto her waist : whilst she
From her white hands the liquid sparkles shook,
And cast them in the air, like diamonds free,
A thousand times more pure, more beautiful to see.

Straightway a swan came sailing up the stream,
To which she call'd, and with a timid grace
It sidled near her—quiet as a dream !
The nymph kept, like a statue, in her place ;
Then sudden stoop'd, and scatter'd in its face
A thousand wave-drops—back it fled in fear,
Ruffled its brilliant feathers from the chase,
Then slowly round its sidelong course did steer,
Stretch'd its broad wings, and boldly darted near !

As flew the swan so flew the maiden fair;
Then caught a scarf, with which the boughs were drest,
And flung it o'er its wings—it sprang in air!
Flash'd the white waters from its panting breast,
Whilst she laugh'd loud, and mock'd its ruffled crest!
Seeming some creature of ethereal birth;
Ere long a butterfly besought her quest—
Up flew the scarf in light and playful mirth,
The butterfly and maid seem'd both too bright for earth!

Lured by the sound of waters, soft and shy
From 'neath the woods, a dappled fawn tripp'd slow;
Gazing askance with ever restless eye,
Until half gain'd the singing stream below;
Anon he listen'd—unresolved to go.
Then did the merry drops in music sink:
Onward he leapt all eager for its flow,
And bent his beauteous head as if to drink,
Unconscious he of nymph close watching at the brink.

Swift flew the scarf—the dappled fawn was caught!
It plunged, it swerved—away the wavelets flew;
With matchless grace the maid her captive brought
Amidst the weeds, and kept it struggling through;

Then tighter round the silken bandage drew:
It rear'd, it leapt!—the stream in fountains spread!
Oh, Love, the sport, the strife, between the two!
At last a rush of waters o'er her head
O'erpower'd the laughing nymph, and free the glad
    fawn fled.

Swift with the racing fawn I hurried thence,
Nor let one breaking branch my haunt betray,
But left to sweetness and to innocence
The Beauty and her bath, and stepp'd away.
Guarded by angels be her sanctuary!
Still her companions prove the swan and fawn,
Still happy with the butterfly to play,
Bathe in the brook, or dance upon the lawn,
Or meet with lips of song the golden grace of dawn.

THE SOUL.

What is the Soul? It may not be
   A light which chance hath waked to birth;
Nor is that power, Necessity,
   The mother of the earth.
Materialists in vain may teach
   That Nature form'd this glorious whole;
In worlds which science cannot reach,
   " God!—God made man a living soul!"

What is the Soul?—A deathless ray—
   A gift of that immortal Hand
Which from blind chaos struck the day,
   And held, unpoised, the sea and land;
Who o'er the earth shed beauty rife,
   Who gave the Elements their might,
Who waked the planets into life,
   And bowed the starry globe of night.

From stern Necessity call *grace*—
  Call *order* from the dreams of chance—
Bid your material god replace
  The heavenly fountain we advance:
The seasons would return no more,
  The erring planets lose their track,
Confusion stalk from shore to shore,
  And Ruin shout to Chaos back!

Can *knowledge*, then, oppress the brain,
  O'erload the reason's glorious might;
Imagination's wing restrain,
  And blind our intellectual sight?—
No: the rivers of the world combined
  Have never fill'd the boundless sea;
And what is ocean to the mind?
  Like time unto eternity!

Not knowledge hath debased the sense,
  But *vice*—that, even in our youth,
Saith to Religion's light—" Go hence!
  I will not, dare not, know the truth!
If I deceive myself, 'tis well:
  Let me live on, and still deceive;
If sinners tread the *brink* of hell,
  'Twere death to TREMBLE and believe!"

O God, the Father of the Soul!
   O Jesus, Saviour of the world!
Bid knowledge spread from pole to pole,
   Be Faith's bright banner wide unfurl'd.
For whatsoe'er the soul may be,
   Or wheresoe'er the soul may dwell,
To live for God's eternity
   Is better than to live for hell!

AN EARLY VISITOR.

The dewy morn, with golden feet,
Came sighing fond, and blushing sweet;
And o'er the casement's flowery stand
Reclined her warm and brilliant hand;
Stole from the rose its rath perfume,
And leapt, all glowing, in the room;
Shook gold upon the carpet round,
Each printed form, with sunthreads bound.
Anon—as if half weary there—
Her golden limbs adorned a chair;
And flashed a hundred brilliant hues
On classic Reynolds' "Tragic Muse;"
Pressed golden kisses o'er the pearl
Of Christall's lovely "Shepherd Girl;"
And, spite of Shakspere's verse of old,
Kept gilding still refinèd gold!—
At last a little over-free,
She threw herself upon my knee;
In beaming glances met my looks,
And blinded me for reading books:

Red, green, or orange spots were all
I found where'er my sight could fall;
'Till, half provoked, I wish'd the maid
Were fairly buried in the shade!
For, jealous of the least advance,
She struck the fire out with a glance;
Then, as with music's gifts to please,
Her sparkling fingers touched the keys!
'Twas something to be seen, not heard,
Too eloquent for note, or word:
Cecilia's hand, though oft admired,
Had ne'er such brilliancy inspired;
Could ne'er intenser gaze enthral;
But then, alas, the touch was all!

So I to business hurried then;
Engagements with commercial men
Sped swift the time; whilst Morn withdrew
To vernal scenes and pleasures new;
Through lanes with honeysuckle sweet,
Through many a sylvan, calm retreat;
Danced with the ripple of the brook,
Still gilding every path she took;
And, oh! till we again may meet,
May Heaven bless those golden feet!

BLAME ME NOT.

They blame this changeless brow of care,
    This silent woe they blame:
They little know how sweet 's despair,
    If it but breathe thy name!
They little think how passing dear
    Is sadness unto me;
How sweet the sorrow, sweet the tear,
    In silence shed for thee!

Life hath no home, no hope, no love—
    The dove hath lost her ark—
The very face of heaven above
    Seems hopeless now and dark:
Yet little think they, still how dear
    Is sadness unto me—
How sweet the sorrow, sweet the tear,
    In silence shed for thee!

THE DEAD SWAN.

(THE STREAM LAMENTETH FOR HER LOST COMPANION.)

Darkly now and lonely
    Night on me descends;
Once and but once only
    We 've been parted friends!
What doth Life inherit
    That can Hope impart?
Oh, sweet Bird, or Spirit,
    Tell me where thou art!

With a troubled feeling
    Came the Night profound;
With a sigh revealing
    Sorrow all around!
Sounds too sad to lose them
    Through the forest crept,
Whilst upon my bosom
    Thou in beauty slept!

Ill could ne'er betide me,
    Through the wildest night;
There thou lay beside me
    Like a beam of light!
Till the dark hour ending,
    To thy happy stream,
Forest deer descending
    Woke thee from thy dream!

Then thy beauty darted
    All its rays of light,
Like a sylph thou started
    In thy sparkling flight!
Whilst the deer—though frighted
    From the water's brink—
Paused, as half delighted,
    And forgot to drink.

O ye Stars, that often
    In my heart have slept,
Fate's decree now soften:
    Long and lone I've wept!
Where is she whose brightness
    Lent the rash delight;
Know ye, in your lightness?
    Answer, Stars of night!

Not a voice repeateth
    Tidings where thou art,
Save the wave that beateth
    O'er my troubled heart;
Save the winds that slowly
    'Neath the sedges rise,
Every feeling holy
    Into silence dies!

Not the stars can bring her
    Back to life and day;
Why should I then linger?
    Waste, poor Stream, away!
What doth Life inherit
    That can Hope impart?
Oh, sweet Bird, or Spirit,
    Tell me where thou art!

THE LOST ONE FOUND.

The mother's hearth is lone, her child hath roam'd away—
A truant from the morning meal, till now the close of day;
And whither he hath wandered, what field-path he hath cross'd,
She knows not, but distractedly is seeking for her *lost!*

He used to play so cheerfully about the cottage-door,
No wanderer after bee and bird—he loved his mother more!
And now, though every spot she'd search'd within the village ground,
She dared not meet her husband's face until his boy was found.

Where wild nuts grow, and blackberries their tempting
    treasure bear,
She sought; she ask'd each cotter's girl—but none had
    seen him there;
She told them of his fair young face, his sunny curls,
    his years;
But when she strove to tell them more, she could not
    for her tears.

Away she sped o'er upland field, and by the orchard
    bank,
Until she near'd a rushy brook, whose bridge was but
    a plank;
And, half afraid to look therein, she hurried o'er and
    found
Two foot-prints small—the mother knelt and kiss'd the
    grassy ground!

Two little foot-prints o'er the bridge, beside the golden
    plain;
And 'midst the grass a flower-crush'd spot as where a
    child had lain;
And scatter'd rushes wild about show'd where his feet
    had stray'd—
Her child had cross'd the dangerous brook, and must
    have reach'd the glade.

The forest glade, that lonesome track, where 'neath dry leaf and weed
The viper hides his venom'd fang, and noxious insects breed;
Where—ah! was that a garment moved? She rush'd into the wood,
Alas! 'twas but the hawthorn gray before whose boughs she stood.

By thicket and wild brake she search'd, but every trace was gone;
It could not be so mere a child thus far had rambled on:
And, sinking down bewilder'd, unknowing how to stir,
She heard a voice, a little voice, but, oh! 'twas bliss to her!

And forth he ran, the truant one, and clasp'd his mother's knees,
Put up his fruit-stain'd lips to kiss, and tried each art to please;
And bade the weeper not to cry, although his own poor cheek
Show'd traces of his day's-long tears in many a piteous streak.

And in that wood the mother sat, and pointed to the sky,
And bade her boy remember Him who 'd watch'd him from on high!
Had sent his influence down to guard his little footsteps there;
So with her child, the mother knelt—and blessed her God in prayer.

TORQUATO TASSO.

[Torquato Tasso, one of the most celebrated poets that Italy ever produced, was born at Sorrento in 1544. His works show him to have been a philosopher, an orator, a logician, a critic, and a poet, excelling in every kind of composition. While he was at the court of Alphonso, Duke of Ferrara, he incurred that prince's anger by his passion for the Princess Leonora of Este, his patron's sister; and being somewhat disordered in his intellect, he was ungenerously shut up in a madhouse for seven years, where he underwent the most illiberal treatment. Tasso himself says that every rigour and inhumanity it is possible to conceive were practised towards him. The remonstrances of several Italian princes at length procured his release; and when Cardinal Aldobrandini ascended the papal chair by the name of Clement VIII., he invited him to Rome, resolving to confer upon him the laureate crown in the Capitol. While, however, the preparations were going on for this ceremony with the greatest magnificence and pomp—promising to be the most splendid pageant beheld in Italy for centuries—Tasso was taken ill, and died in 1595.]

'TWAS in the minstrel clime of Italy,
The hour which marries twilight to the stars;
When Memory speaks to Beauty, and the air
Seems languishing for silence; at that hour,

Beside a classic fount, whose broken arch
Portray'd the poet's fortune, Tasso slept.
The dying day oft through the parted clouds
Shot sudden gleams, and o'er the slumberer's cheek
Now light, now shadow swept; and haply these
Might touch or influence the poet's dream;
For, as he said, two spirits sought his side,
And each, alternate, pictured to his mind
Visions immortal. Fame and Truth were they,
And thus address'd the poet's slumbering ear :—

SPIRIT OF FAME.

It is the voice of Fame
    Which greets thee on her flight;
The star that shall illume thy name
    Now trembles into light:
Around thee glories wait
    In long triumphal line;
The classic throne, its crown and state,
    Laurel and lyre, are thine.

Thrill, soul of song, with fire!
    Pour, heart of love, thy lay!
Hopes that immortal minds inspire
    Shed triumph on thy way.

The eternal hours prolong
　　The music of thy name ;
Wake, Tasso, wake ! thou heir of song !
　　It is the voice of Fame.

SPIRIT OF TRUTH.

Avoid that syren voice,
　　Shun the betrayer's tongue ;
When did the laurel e'er rejoice
　　One victim heart of song !
Soar thou the topmost height,
　　Attain the classic leaf,
But know the hours of loftiest flight
　　Are ever the most brief.

Go, waste thy bloom of years
　　To grace a monarch's state,
And nourish Fame's frail flowers with tears,
　　And learn repentance late !
Go, court the vain of earth,
　　Seek praise from Beauty's eyes ;
Then learn how little is the worth
　　Of that thy soul did prize !

SPIRIT OF FAME.

Oh, charm'd thy lyre shall be,
    And fill'd with power to move
The loftiest minds to chivalry,
    The noblest hearts to love;
And they on whose renown
    A nation's shouts attend
Shall be the first thy lyre to crown,
    The first to call thee friend.

The tournament and feast,
    The banquet and the ball,
These of thine honours shall be least,
    Thy fame transcend them all:
The proud and princely throng
    Shall worship at thy shrine,
Assert the sovereignty of song,
    And own its gifts divine.

SPIRIT OF TRUTH.

Oh, fickle is the breath
    Of popular acclaim;
And purchased often but by death
    Is an illustrious name!

TORQUATO TASSO.

Fame, like the rainbow's glow,
    Is but the type of tears;
And Glory's harvest, like the snow,
    Dissolves and disappears.

The envy and the scorn,
    The penury and pain—
Oh, better hadst thou ne'er been born
    Than wake the poet's strain!
That voice doth but deceive:
    Avoid ambition's goal,
Nor let the fire of fancy leave
    Its ashes on thy soul.

SPIRIT OF FAME.

Great Rome shall hail thee son!
    Link'd with the glorious twain,
With triumphs Ariosto won,
    With Dante's matchless strain;
For unto thee are given
    The thoughts that angels breathe;
And Tasso's song of heaven
    The light of hosts shall wreathe.

The loveliest of the land,
  The high-born and the young,
Shall deem it fame to kiss the hand
  That wrote Jerusalem's song.
Shake off this soulless thrall,
  And arm for victory's field;
When beauty, love, and glory call,
  Can Tasso's spirit yield?

SPIRIT OF TRUTH.

Hark! 'tis the captive's shriek,
  A voice that loads the air
With wrongs too terrible to speak,
  With madness and despair.
It tells of genius lost,
  Of beauty unattain'd,
Of love pursued at reason's cost,
  Of glory sunk and stain'd.

Dimm'd is that noble mind
  That wing'd to heaven its flight;
The frenzied eyes, far worse than blind,
  Blaze with delirious light:
That hand, the Muse inspired,
  'Gainst phantom-horror strives;

Now starts from hell's imagined fires,
   Now flees the maniac's gyves.

SPIRIT OF FAME.

The imperial streets resound,
   Rome's banners wave on high,
And garlands belt the classic ground,
   As though a king swept by.
The hero-bard ascends
   His coronation throne;
And hark! is that a shout which rends
   Those oracles of stone?

The choral voices float
   In hymns of joy and praise,
Cittern, and lyre, and clarion note,
   Their lofty triumph raise;
The Capitolian throng
   With music sound thy name;
Wake, Tasso, wake! thou heir of song!
   It is the voice of Fame.

SPIRIT OF TRUTH.

By St. Onofrio's shrine
   Dark sounds of grief arise;

And weeping eyes in woe decline
    Where a dying minstrel lies.
Ah, what are shows or state
    To that pale drooping head?
The tardy triumph comes too late
    Which comes to crown the dead.

Can Rome's proud chaplets now
    One meed of grace impart?
Can Fame relieve the anguish'd brow,
    Or bind the broken heart?
With misery rack'd and bow'd
    Illustrious Tasso lies ;
And what avail the applauding crowd,
    Or shouts that rend the skies?

And is 't for this reward
    Thou 'lt spend thy soul's rich power!
Alas, unhappy bard,
    Thine is a fatal dower!
Yet when were hearts e'er found
    By Fame's proud breath unstirr'd?
Woe that *Delusion* should be crown'd,
    And *Truth* so little heard!

ADAM.

"And God created Man in His own image."

The Mind is victor over Time;
   The dial of the brain
Points not to hours, but years sublime,
   That o'er oblivion reign!
Immortal as its primal source,
It scatters centuries in its course—
   Explores the worlds of thought;
Nor folds its heav'n-enfranchised wing,
Till reach'd that intellectual spring
   Which crowns the shore it sought!

The Spirit of the Past appears—
   The Present fades—is gone!
The feelings of unnumber'd years
   Are centred into one!
A radiance o'er my vision glows,
While spreads that Eden of repose

Ere Sorrow's sway began;
I see that morn, whose light unfurl'd,
Woke the first Sabbath of the world
    Upon the soul of man!

No cloud hangs o'er the far serene,
    Earth smiles amidst her flowers,
As though that moment GOD had been
    In her Elysian bowers!
Yet holier than the earth or sky,
A presence born of Deity,
    With grace-illumined brow,
Glorious, as from JEHOVAH's hands,
The parent of earth's millions stands
    Before my vision now.

Erect—ere sin had bow'd his frame,
    And struck his forehead dim;
Ere, exiled to eternal shame
    By swords of cherubim,
He heard the voice of GOD complain—
Saw branded on the brow of Cain
    The mark with murder red;
Knew all the horrors guilt must know,
Which, like an avalanche of woe,
    Swept ruin on his head!

I mark those lineaments divine,
    In their immortal bloom;
Unmarr'd by one degrading line
    Prophetic of their doom;
I gaze—and back the steeds of thought,
Midst years of blood one act had wrought;
    Then trace the steps of time
Through all that sad mortality—
The universe of graves to be—
    From flood, disease, and crime!

The cities of the earth display
    Their toil-oppressed race;
Merit neglected on her way,
    Whilst Pride usurps her place:
There lies the plague-polluted corse,—
Envy, and Hatred, and Remorse,
    The Passions' burning flow;
There lurks Revenge with poinard bare—
Terror that darkens to despair—
    And Infamy, and Woe!

Where now is that imperial form,
    That majesty of glance,
That brow o'er which the soul's wild storm
    Of passions ne'er advance?—

Alas for Sin!—Through ages past
Mark Adam's seed in sorrow cast,
   Still mourners upon earth :—
Then, on the Cross of Calvary,
Thy crucified Redeemer see,
   And learn Man's second birth.

Rise! rise! ye everlasting spheres,
   And wake the hymn of life!
Praise Him, ye *Eighteen Hundred Years*
   With man's salvation rife!
Though sin, and woe, and death prevail,
The Rock of Ages shall not fail
   Whilst Faith on earth may dwell;
The soul baptised in Christ shall rise
Triumphant to its native skies,
   Despite the powers of hell!

WAITING FOR THE COUNTESS.

(FROM LANDSEER'S DRAWING OF LADY BLESSINGTON'S
FAVOURITE HOUND.)

'Tis sweet to watch the morning break
    O'er mountains bleak and bare,
To view the clouds, like vessels, take
    The azure sea of air!
To watch morn's magic pencil touch
    Each golden stream and grove;—
And sweet it is, when loving much,
    To wait for her we love.

Man *speaks* of "friendship, faith, and truth,"
    But oft his *acts* declare
His friendship is a dream of youth,
    His faith a thing of air!
And if an honest heart on earth
    Is really to be found,
'Tis not so oft in *human* worth
    As in the worthier hound!

WAITING FOR THE COUNTESS.

Oh! never knight to ladye bright,
    Nor bard's impassion'd breath,
Nor cavalier in maiden's ear,
    Ere seem'd more true to death
Than this half-reasoning, noble brute,
    That puts Man's truth to shame;
This creature—eloquent though mute!—
    And friend—in more than name!

Thou, loved as genius must be loved;
    And famed as beauty's famed;
Admired wherever thou hast moved,
    Renown'd wherever named;
Not one of all the friends thou 'st found,
    Whose words and looks were sweet,
Ere loved thee better than this hound
    That waits thy coming feet!

Rank—station—beauty—what are all,
    If all yet fail to win
A heart still true to friendship's call,
    Still warm with love within?
Oh, Life is lone, and little worth,
    Unless affection meet
A faithfulness like his on earth,
    That waits thy coming feet!

YOUTH AND AGE.

The proudest poetry of youth
   Is—" Would I were a Man!"
The golden years that lie between
   Youth, like a dream, would span:
'Tis in its thought—'tis in its heart—
   'Tis ever on its tongue;
But oh, the poetry of age,
   It is—"*When I was young!*"

Thus, in the morn of life, our feet
   Would distant pathways find;
The sun still face to face we meet—
   The shadow falls behind!
But when the morn of life is o'er,
   And Nature grows less kind;
The length'ning shadow creeps before—
   The sunlight falls behind!

With many a murmur, slow and sad,
    The stream of life flows on;
That which we prized not when we had
    Is doubly prized when gone!
And many a sad and solemn truth
    Lies written on life's page;
Between the " Poetry of Youth!"
    And " Poetry of Age!"

RIVA DI SAN MARCO.

[It must be borne in mind that the legend which we are about to produce is recorded by more than one authentic chronicler, and that it was sufficiently believed to give birth to a public religious ceremony. In the year 1341, an inundation of many days' continuance had raised the water three cubits higher than it had ever before been seen in Venice; and during a stormy night, while the flood appeared to be still increasing, a poor old fisherman sought what refuge he could find by mooring his bark close to the Riva di San Marco. The storm was yet raging, when three persons approached, and offered him a good fare if he would convey them to the two castles of Sido. Scarcely had they gained the strait, when they saw a galley, rather flying than sailing up the Adriatic, manned (if we may so say) with devils, who seemed hurrying, with fierce and threatening gestures, to sink Venice in the deep. The strangers conjured the fiends to depart: at the word, the demoniacal galley vanished, and the three holy passengers were quietly landed. "Go to the Doge," said one, "and the procuratori, and assure them that, but for we three, Venice would have been drowned. I am St. Mark; my two comrades are St. George and St. Nicholas." On the morrow the fisherman did as he was told, and he not only received his fare, but an annual pension to boot. Moreover, a solemn procession and thanksgiving were appointed, in gratitude to the three holy corpses which had rescued from such calamity the land affording them burial.—*Abridged from Sketches of Venetian History.*]

Thrice honour'd be St. Nicholas, St. George, and good
    St. Mark,
And blessings on the fisherman who steer'd the gallant
    bark;

When lower'd the mighty firmament—one black fore-
    dooming page :—
And wild and high the waves howl'd by, foaming and
    white with rage!

The thunders clamour'd to the blast, the lightnings
    flash'd about,
Like flaming brands by demons forged amidst that
    hellish rout;
The proudest halls of Venice rock'd unto their very base,
And mothers gazed in agony upon their children's face.

Still eastward swept the sainted bark, and smote the
    billows back,
Calm as the eagle floats along its cloud-beleaguer'd
    track;
The whirlwind own'd the spirit-grasp of some superior
    sway,
And, shrieking, vanish'd like a fiend defeated of its
    prey!

Then gazed the aged fisherman upon the glorious three,
And moved the helm with trembling hand, and mar-
    vell'd silently;
For rays of light upon his sight in angel-beauty gleam'd
From brows more eminently fair than poet's fancy
    dream'd!

Now blacker vapours choked the breath, and sadder sights appear'd,
As through the Adriatic strait the venturous vessel steer'd !
A galley throng'd with demons foul was scudding o'er the wave,
Which deeper grew, and faster flew, at every sign they gave !

And horrid conjurations there, and curses long and wild,
Doom'd to the last and worst despair, mother, and sire, and child !
Devoted towers, and palaces, and temples, to that tide
Whose dreadful billows leap'd around in their tempestuous pride !

But lo ! the sacred bark wore on, the galley shook with dread,
The demons stretch'd their wings of flame, and howling, turn'd and fled !
The horrors of that spectral sea at once were put to flight,
As the morning stole, like a parting soul, from the grave of the buried night !

Joy! joy for Venice!—fast and far the song of gladness flows;
The grateful mother clasps her child, and half forgets her woes:
The sea hath moan'd itself to sleep within the tranquil bay,
And sunny is the welcome sky, and beautiful its ray!

Now bid the voice of prayer arise, and wreathe the holy shrine,
For shielded hath our city been by influence divine!
Thanksgiving to the Virgin pour beside this hallow'd bark;
And glory to St. Nicholas, St. George, and good St. Mark!

THE ANGEL'S CALL.

IN MEMORY OF
JULIANA ANNE TAVARÉ.

To the green grave newly made,
   Sisters come!
To the churchyard where she's laid,
   Sisters come!
When the ninth day downward dips
Will the spirit leave her lips;—
   Bear her home!
Earth and shroud may then be spared,—
Angels have her house prepared,—
   Bear her home!

She was purer than the morn,
   Sisters come!
Spotless as a flower new born,
   Sisters come!

All who saw her near could part
'Till her image fill'd each heart,—
<blockquote>Bear her home!</blockquote>
Never death kiss'd maiden's eyes
Fitter for our Father's skies,—
<blockquote>Bear her home!</blockquote>

There is grief with her to part,—
<blockquote>Sisters come!</blockquote>
Anguish in the Mother's heart,—
<blockquote>Sisters come!</blockquote>
Teach the mourner's faith to rise
To that Mansion in the skies,
<blockquote>Where she's gone;</blockquote>
Teach the Mother's lips to say,
'Mid the tears that must have way,
<blockquote>*Thy will be done!*</blockquote>

ALL THINGS FOR GOOD.

Nothing we see, but is for good;
   No sight, no shape throughout creation,
But hath, if rightly understood,
   Some wise and spiritual relation.

Throughout all worlds, throughout all time,
   The outer of the inner telleth;
Each seed is but a germ sublime,
   Where wisdom, love, and beauty dwelleth.

And I can ne'er the thought forego
   That flowers, and trees, and all that groweth,
Have sympathy with hearts below,
   And love the hand that love bestoweth.

Who knows how link by link we draw
   The slender chain which life enforces?—
A drop of dew may show some law,
   That guides the planets in their courses.

Perchance the very sand we pass
	May teach a truth without our seeing;
And e'en a simple blade of grass
	Proclaim the Universal Being.

THE FLOWER SPIRIT.

When earth was in its golden prime,
    Ere grief or gloom had marr'd its hue,
And Paradise, unknown to crime,
    Beneath the love of angels grew,
Each flower was then a spirit's home,
    Each tree a living shrine of song;
And, oh! that ever hearts could roam—
    Could quit for sin that seraph throng!

But there the spirit lingers yet,
    Though dimness o'er our visions fall;
And flowers that seem with dewdrops wet
    Weep angel-tears for human thrall;
And sentiments and feelings move
    The soul, like oracles divine;
All hearts that ever bow'd to love
    First found it by the flowers' sweet shrine.

A voiceless eloquence and power,
    Language that hath in life no sound
Still haunts, like Truth, the Spirit-flower,
    And hallows even Sorrow's ground.
The wanderer gives it Memory's tear,
    Whilst home seems pictured on its leaf;
And hopes, and hearts, and voices dear,
    Come o'er him—beautiful as brief.

'Tis not the bloom, though wild or rare,
    It is the spirit power within,
Which melts and moves our souls, to share
    The Paradise we here might win.
For Heaven itself around us lies,
    Not far, not yet our reach beyond,
And we are watch'd by angel's eyes,
    With hope and faith still fond!

I well believe a spirit dwells
    Within the flower! least changed of all
That of the pass'd Immortal tells—
    The glorious meeds before man's fall;
Yet, still, though I should never see
    The mystic grace within it shine—
Its essence is sublimity,
    Its feeling all divine.

THE SHIP OF HEAVEN.

A DREAM.

———

'Tis day, but sun or sky
   No human eye may see;
Like a mighty shroud, the heavy air
   Hangs dim and drearily!

'Tis day—yet on the rock
   The falcon sits forlorn,
Awaiting, cold and restlessly,
   The coming of the morn.

A ray, as of the sun,
   Flashes along the deep,
And, hark! dull whispers of the blast
   Through the old forest sweep.

Yet all is calm, as lull'd
   By some magician's wand:
It is no sun that lights the deep—
   No blast that sweeps the land!

Like mountains that have been
    By ancient tempests riven,
Opens in wild sublimity
    The lofty arch of heaven!

The giant clouds dissolve
    Mysteriously away,
As darkness melts to radiance
    Before the power of day.

Innumerable beams
    Of variegated light
Burst, from that everlasting sphere,
    Upon my tranced sight.

Temples of living fire,
    Mild as the lunar ray—
Fountains that overflow with stars,
    Shine up the open way!

Suddenly, from the vault,
    Like lightning when storms rave,
A bow of atmospheric hues
    Spans the vast heaven and wave.

A Ship!—a heavenly Ship!—
    Her sails are clouds of snow,
Fine as the summer moon shines through,
    On pleasant eves below.

From the miraculous cleft
  She takes her beauteous flight;
And launching on the tide of air,
  Speeds down the waves of light.

Gushes the trumpet's breath
  With organ melody;—
And, at the sound, ten thousand shapes
  Spring from the groaning sea!

The sea gives up its dead—
  Its brave, its honour'd dead;
Their thronging footsteps press the deck,
  But soundless is their tread!

The aged and wither'd brow,
  The stately and the fair,
The warrior-knight and lowly hind—
  The prince and slave—meet there.

They gaze on me, with eyes
  That evermore dilate,
As if with the thin gelid air
  Engross'd—incorporate.

Their forms glide, like star-rays
  Upon a rapid stream—
Pale, shadowy, changeful—still in all
  Identical they seem!

Again the Ship of Heaven
    Her wondrous path doth take;
Silently she moves o'er the sea—
    Her vast stern leaves no wake!

Vain is my wish to move:
    A ponderous column, bound
With demon-chains upon my breast,
    Confines me to the ground.

Vain is my hope to speak:
    Language denies the power
To tell the bitter agony—
    The terror of this hour!

'Tis past!—back to my heart
    The fever'd blood springs, now,
And the illusions of dark sleep
    Fast leave my aching brow!

THE EVE OF ST. JOHN.

She waiteth by the forest stream,—
　　She sitteth on the ground;
While the moonlight, like a mantle,
　　Wraps her tenderly around!
She sitteth through the cold, cold night,
　　But not a step draws near,
Though *his* name is on her trembling lips,
　　His voice meets not her ear!

Hist! was 't the haunted stream that spoke?
　　What droning sound swept there?
She listens!—still no human tone
　　O'erhears she anywhere!—
Oh! was 't the forest bough that took
　　That sad and spectral mien?
She looketh round distractedly,
　　But there is nothing seen!

Dark, in the quiet moonlight,
    Her shadowy form is thrown;
With a strange and lonely mournfulness,
    It seems not like her own!
She glanceth o'er her shoulder fair,
    The moon is gleaming wide;
She turneth—JESU! what is there
    Pale sitting by her side?

She pauseth for a single breath—
    She hearkens for a tone;
And terror pains her chilling veins,
    For breath or sound—is none!
The silence—oh, it racks her brain,
    It binds it like a chord!
She 'd given worlds though but to hear
    The chirping of a bird!

The shadow rose before her—
    It stood upon the stream:
" O blessed shadow, ease my soul,
    And tell me 'tis a dream!
Thou tak'st the form of one they vow'd
    Mine eyes should see no more!"
The shadow stood across the stream,
    And beckon'd pale before.

The shadow beckon'd on before,
    Yet deign'd her no reply;
The ladye rose, and straight the stream
    To its pebbly breast was dry!
It pass'd the wood—it cross'd the court—
    The gate flew from its chain—
The gentle ladye knew she stood
    Within her own domain!

And still the awful shadow glid,
    Without or breath or tone,
Until it came to a sullen sluice
    'Mid yellow sand and stone,
But the rock and sand disdain'd to stand,
    The water scorn'd to flow;
Thus blood was seen down the rift between,
    And the dead reveal'd below.

The dead was seen, in the space between,
    And the ladye knew it well!
She kiss'd its cheek with a piercing shriek,
    With a woe no tongue may tell,
The gory shadow beckon'd on,
    And still her steps implored;
But she follow'd not, for on that spot
    She found a shiver'd sword.

She grasp'd the hilt—its silken thread
    Her own fair skill had wove;
A brother's hand had struck the dead—
    His sword had slain her love!
She took the corpse upon her knees,
    Its cheek lay next her own;
Like sculpture fair, in the moonlight there,
    Like misery turn'd to stone!

*   *   *   *   *   *

No food to seek for the raven's beak—
    The gibbet serves them true,
With young, and sweet, and dainty meat,
    As e'er the ravens knew;
And few they see near the gibbet-tree,
    For a bleeding form glides on,
From the haunted stream, in the moon's cold beam,
    On the Eve of good Saint John!

NOT TO-NIGHT.

There 's a shadow falling
    In the moonlit street;
There 's a fond voice calling,
    Calling low, and sweet:
To and from the window,
    To and from the gate;
Half resolved to enter,
    Half inclined to wait!
While the chimes of midnight
    Float upon the gale;
Thus the shadow passeth
    In the moonlight pale.

Brightly in the cottage
    Burns the Christmas fire;
Round its flame are seated
    Daughter, son, and sire:

Oft a glance is centred
    On the casement pane;
Oft a step is ventured,
    Then returns again.
Still the shadow falleth,
    Still the moments go,
Still that low voice calleth
    How to let him know!

Two lights in the window,
    One light on the stair;
Well the Watcher knoweth
    Wherefore they are there!
Slowly—very slowly—
    'Neath the moonlight ray,
Passeth voice and shadow,
    From the path away:
While the chimes of midnight
    Following still his feet,
Whisper of the morrow,
    When they two may meet.

PRIZES AND BLANKS.

The prizes in the wheel of chance
    Are thrown by some blind elf;
But he, who would through life advance,
    Must turn the wheel himself!
Why wait for Fortune's hand to bring
    What thine can well achieve?
The worker at the wheel can sing,
    Whilst Folly's victims grieve!
    Then let the treach'rous wheel of chance
        Be turn'd by imp or elf;
    The man that would through life advance
        Must turn the wheel himself!

There is a seed within the breast
    That blooms, and fills the soul
With joy and sweetness unexprest;
    A prize—worth Fortune's whole!

It is the seed Employment sets ;
   It brightens hours of gloom ;
And he who rears it, ne'er regrets
   The toil that bids it bloom !
     Then let the treach'rous wheel of chance
       Be turn'd by imp or elf;
     The man that would through life advance
       Must turn the wheel himself !

Who knowledge hath and skill to use,
   And on his work depends ;
Though Fortune may her smiles refuse,
   His fingers are his friends !
The very effort to improve
   Life's bare and stunted plan,
Is in itself a work of love
   And lifts the heart of man !
     Then let the treach'rous wheel of chance
       Be turned by imp or elf;
     The man that would through life advance
       Must turn the wheel himself !

THE TEMPLE.

Know'st thou the temple of Song?
   The harps of all Nations are there
The hymn, and the anthem, and song,
   God's voice and the music of prayer!
The visions of ages surround
   That temple of beauty and grace;
And the stream that encircles the ground
   Reflects in each wavelet a face!

Know'st thou the temple of Song!
   Lov'st thou its banner of fame!
Where is the being whose tongue
   Speaks not in praise of its name?
While spirits with liberty glow—
   While hearts with affection are rife—
The song of that temple shall flow,
   And its voice be the music of life.

THE HEART.

Oh, the Heart is a troublesome thing !
   Its fancies and follies are more
Than the dews which fall round us in spring,
   Or the wind-beaten sands of the shore :
Though fed upon kindness—it pines
   The moment you wander away ;
It is merry as long as Life shines—
   As long as Love smiles it is gay !
Then pause ere you threaten to part,
   Reflect ere you bid it adieu ;
Ah ! what can one do with a Heart
   So fond, yet so changeable, too ?

One moment inconstant and vain,
   Its follies the kindest would try ;
The next, if it see but your pain,
   To solace that pain it would die !

Then oft it each feeling employs
  In seeking new ways to excel,
And angels might envy the joys
  In the core of its being that dwell:
So pause ere you threaten to part,
  Reflect ere you bid it adieu;
Ah! what can one do with a Heart
  So fond, yet so changeable, too?

THE CAPTIVE.

There was joy in my home—there was beauty and light,
For, fair as their mother first smiled on my sight,
My daughters around me in innocence bloom'd,
And my sons the free bearing of manhood assumed;
While Christmas came round with mirth, music, and song,
And their sire was the proudest of all that gay throng.

But a sound filled the land with suspicion and dread,
And the guiltless from home to a prison were led!
From the arms of my children they tore me away,
No anguish could move them—no mercy had they!
And Christmas came round—but, ah! changed were its strains,
To the clank of my fetters—to darkness and chains!

And years crept away; still I hoped, as of yore,
To behold my sweet home—kiss my children once more!

Whilst a record of days midst the darkness I kept,
I prayed to the GOD of the captive, and wept!
Till memory grew wearied, and blighted its power,
And Christmas came round, and I knew not the hour!

Still years and years fled—no impression they gave;
'Twas a void, a delirium, a life in the grave—
A chaos of thought—a dream, wild yet awake;
But, alas! such a dream as no morning could break;
And Christmas came round, but its brightness was o'er;
It found not the captive, he knew it no more!

At last, when the hairs on my temples were gray,
When my form had grown feeble and bent with decay,
The door of my cell grated open—for me!
I was dragg'd into day and there told I was free!
It was winter: the wind whistled cold o'er my brow;
But methought it seem'd Christmas, and welcomed its
    snow!

I was free! I beheld the glad sun once again;
Though its light was but torture—its loveliness pain.
I was free! I forgot the sad years that had roll'd;
I forgot I was poor, and decrepid, and old!
And methought that sweet Christmas again would
    appear
In the home of my heart, with the beings most dear!

I drew towards the spot where my home used to bloom ;
But its walls lay in dust, and my wife in the tomb !
My daughters were scatter'd the wild waters wide,
And my sons midst the wars for their country had died !
So I turn'd to the dungeon, and craved for my chains,
For the captive no home and no Christmas remains !

EARTHLY BEAUTY.

There was an angel loved the flowers,
    Who brought them dew from sainted springs;
And came with heaven's own glowing hours
    Upon her white and sparkling wings;
Then sat enamour'd all the morn,
    Lone gazing on her bower of bliss;
For, oh! she thought Love's self was born
    In some sweet paradise like this.

And all her fond affections grew
    In beauty round her flowery bands.
That seem'd almost as if they knew
    Their buds were fed by angel hands.
And thus she half forgot the sky,
    Such feeling warm'd her spirit fair!
Till one by one they droop'd to die,
    And left the angel weeping there.

"Alas!" she mourn'd, "who love could place—
　Who let the heart's affections rest
On forms that have such heavenly grace,
　Yet fade away when loved the best?
Alas! that beauty such as thine
　Should die, O Earth, and love deplore!
From thee I wing my way divine,
　Where beauty blooms for evermore."

DESPONDENCY.

Why thus cast down and grieved?
    Why anxious ever?
Is boding Care believed,
    And sweet Hope never?
Look, ere the day's amount
    Of woes confound thee,—
Look up, sad heart, and count
    Thy friends around thee.

Stars, which the Day conceals,
    Shine on unheeded;
'Tis only Night reveals
    How much they're needed!
Is there no heavenly fount
    Whose dews have found thee?
Look up, sad heart, and count
    God's *blessings* round thee.

FAITHFUL AND FAITHLESS.

A little knot of summer flowers
   Hung drooping o'er the streamlet side;
But ah! the sear and sultry hours
   The shallow rippling stream had dried!
So many a trust on earth is lost—
   So many a human friend deceives:
The flow'rets found it to their cost,
   In wasted bloom and wither'd leaves.

In vernal hope and love they grew,
   And, twined in one another, thought
That whilst the breath of life they drew,
   The stream would feed them as it ought!
And yet, alas! for earthly trust,
   For all reliances below,
Their roots were pining in the dust,
   And still the stream no aid could show!

But, like a blessing o'er the plain,
   The morn on wings of cloud descends;
And fast and fresh the bounteous rain
   To every thirsting leaflet sends!
Then woke the flowers to second birth;
   A second life to them was given:
Oh, mortal, is thy trust on earth?
   Then change thy heart, and trust in Heaven!

ANGELS.

Though the beauty of Eden hath wither'd and fled,
   And Angels may visit Man's pathway no more;
Oh, still o'er our lot is their influence shed,
   With a feeling as radiant and sweet as of yore!
Yes; Angels, bright Angels, still hallow our sight,
   Still speak to our souls thro' the dreams of the night!

Not fled, and for ever, the bloom of those days;
   A shadow of glory yet mantles our birth;
For Seraphs smile over the child as he strays—
   And Heaven is beaming around us on Earth!
Yes; Angels, bright Angels, still hallow our sight,
   Still speak to our souls thro' the dreams of the night!

LOVE THEE?

Love thee?—if thou wert but a song
    I 'd learnt in earlier day,
Thou ne'er shouldst leave my lips for long,
    Be from my thought away!
No; thou shouldst be my theme at morn,
    My bird of love at noon;
And I—the happiest lover born—
    Would let none list that tune!

In every stream I 'd hear thee, love,
    In every fountain-fall;
The birds around, the stars above—
    Oh, thou shouldst live in all!
The last sweet rose that dew might sip,
    In summer's fading breath,
Should hear that song upon my lip,
    Companion sweet in death!

If thou wert nothing but a voice
    In Memory's pensive ear,
Still wouldst thou be my only choice—
    A sound for ever dear.
But loving, blooming, all mine own,
    And all Life's bliss to prove,
How couldst thou, in so sad a tone,
    E'er question if I love?

MY LIFE WAS LIKE A FOUNTAIN.

My life was like a fountain
    From Nature's heart that flows,
And ripples down the mountain,
    Still singing as it goes;
The flowers sprang all around it,
    The sun illumed its way:
The lark's glad music found it
    And every wave was gay!

My life was like a garden,
    Where Love would often roam;
And Time sit down and tell me
    Of some ideal home!—
Some home that true affection
    And youthful Hope might win;
With roses climbing o'er it,
    And happy hearts within!

My life was like a rainbow,
    That even out of storm
Could gather tints of beauty,
    Some arch of hope to form !
But now the fount hath taken
    A wider, darker shore ;
Love's garden is forsaken !
    Life's golden light is o'er.

THE FALSE ONE.

And it could please a vacant hour
   To woo him, win him, to thy side;
Play with his heart as with a flower,
   Then change, and all his hopes deride:
And it was triumph to impart
   Such woe as language ne'er exprest;
Oh shame upon the cruel art
   Which thus could wound one human breast!

Though thou wert beauteous as the ray
   That beam'd on Eden's bower of yore;
Though thou wert . . . oh, away, away!
   May heart of man ne'er love thee more!
Would that the angel-hand of Truth
   Might straight unveil thy syren brow;
Disrobe thee of thy bloom of youth,
   And show thee false, as thou art now!

We had been brothers in those years
    Ere life as yet had known a shade;
And I could weep unmanly tears
    To see the wreck thy arts have made.
But go!—assume thy gayest dress—
    Sport lightly with the pleasures nigh;
Why shouldst thou wear one smile the less
    Because a breaking heart must die!

BALLAD.

"Why leave ye thus your father's hall,
    And hie to the gate so oft?"
"'Tis only to watch the moonlight fall
    O'er the waves that sleep so soft."
"And why do ye seek one small blue flower
    Through every sylvan spot?"
"Oh, 'tis but a gem for a maiden's bower,
    A little 'forget-me-not!'"

"Why wear ye that wreath so dim and dry,
    With its leaves all pined and dead?"
The maid look'd up with a tearful eye,
    But never a word she said.
"And why for every word ye speak
    Have ye twenty sighs of late?"
The maiden hath hied, with a blushing cheek,
    Again to the moonlit gate.

Hark! is it a sound indeed that rings—
    A hoof o'er the wild road press'd?
Oh, is it her own true knight that springs,
    And folds her to his breast?
And is it that wreath so dark and dry
    That meets her knight's fond kiss?
Again was a tear in the maiden's eye,
    But, oh! 'twas a tear of bliss!

WILL HE COME?

The snow is falling deeply,
    The wintry winds blow drear.
The gloomy day is waning,
    And yet he is not here!
The old lamp in the casement
    But dimly throws its light;
The way is wild and lonely—
    Do you think he'll come to-night?

A step is on the snow-path,
    A hand is at the door;
A voice—I know each whisper—
    And love it more and more:
He *comes*—though dark the hill-side,
    And long its weary height:
You know I never doubted,
    I *said* he'd come to-night.

THE CAMP IS UP!

The camp is up, 'tis break of day!
    The drums arousing beat,
The signal trumpet's martial bray,
    The tramp of myriad feet,
Still call me from thy last fond kiss,
    And all I deem divine!
For, not in Heaven, where beauty is,
    Can be such charms as thine!

'Twas not the drum—'twas but the gale
    That beat the troubled air;
The trumpet!—'twas the eagle's wail
    Above her rocky lair!
But go—if fame be greater bliss,
    If honour brighter shine—
I'll ask the stars what glory is,
    And that I'll say is thine!

Though Morn's sweet breath doth bid us part,
    And earth and sky seem fair,
Yet night, deep night, is in this heart—
    There is no morning there!
But go—if over love and youth
    Still darkly fortune lowers,
We'll ask the Angels what is truth,
    And that we'll say is ours!

LITTLE THINGS.

Do something for each other,
    Though small the help may be;
There's comfort oft in little things,
    Far more than others see!
It takes the sorrow from the eye,
    It leaves the world less bare,
If but a friendly hand come nigh,
    When friendly hands are rare!
Then cheer the hearts which toil each hour,
    Yet find it hard to live;
And though but little's in our power,
    That little let us give.

The poorest hand, if earnest,
    Some service may achieve;
The humblest voice, if kindly,
    Some sorrow may relieve:

We reck not how the aged poor
  Drag on from day to day,
When e'en the little that they need
  Costs more than they can pay !
Then cheer the hearts that toil each hour,
  Yet find it hard to live ;
And though but little 's in our power
  That little let us give.

SOIL OF ENGLAND.

I BLESS thee, soil of England!
    Where'er thy power prevails;
A grandeur robes thy greenwood—
    A glory crowns thy dales!
Oh, place me wheresoe'er ye will,
    With but *one sod* of thine,—
And Freedom's self shall hallow it,
    As 'twere her native shrine!

And Eloquence shall wreathe that soil
    With England's proudest name;
And Nelson's spirit start therefrom,
    In all its naval fame!
A sound shall thrill that sod of Earth
    As swept a host to war;
And Wellington's unconquer'd sword
    Gleam o'er it like a star!

Yes ; all that elevates the soul
    To things of higher worth ;
The genius of my Native Land
    Would grace that treasured Earth !
I need no charm of mount or vale,
    No glimpse of England's sea—
A shred of her immortal soil
    Is eloquent to me !

MARY.

The daisy loves the hilly mead,
    The lark loves well to nestle by it;
The fawn by mountain stream to feed,
    And crop the sweet flowers springing by it!
All living things are fond of change,
    All tastes—and all affections—vary;
Save mine—but mine—mine never range!
    For I love nothing but my Mary!

The primrose loves the hawthorn hedge,
    The hawthorn loves to bend above it;
The lily, 'midst the river sedge,
    Makes every eye that sees it, love it!
The linnet loves the peep of morn,
    And sings his song in circles airy;
But I—since first my love was born—
    Have loved but one—and that was Mary!

Her cheek is like a snowy cloud,
  With rosy light just breaking through it;
Her eyes are blue—deep blue—and proud,
  As they were glorious eyes, and knew it!
Her lips—shy lips—'tis bliss to woo;
  Her teeth—were presents from some fairy;
But stay! perchance you'll love her, too;
  And none but I must love my Mary!

THINKING OF OTHER DAYS.

I was thinking of days, dearest Mary,
  When we met on those long summer eves,
And the flowers took you, love, for some fairy,
  So lightly you tripp'd o'er their leaves!
But now 'tis a mem'ry of sorrow,
  To muse over joys that are o'er;
Though beauty may come with the morrow,
  There's a beauty it brings me no more!
Where pleasure once smiled there is aching,
  Each month passes by like a year;
And my heart if it be not now breaking.
  May break but too soon, Mary dear,
    Mary dear,
  May break but too soon, Mary dear.

Since the hour, the sad hour, of thy leaving,
  The village has ne'er look'd the same;
The flowers seem as if they were grieving,
  The winds as if sighing thy name!

I roam through the ev'ning dejected,
   I call for a letter in vain;
Each spot that thy fancy selected
   I wander again and again!
Where pleasure once smiled there is aching,
   Each month passes by like a year,
And my heart, if it be not now breaking,
   May break but too soon, Mary dear,
      Mary dear,
   May break but too soon, Mary dear.

LET NOBODY KNOW.

Ah! long is the light
   Of the warm summer day,
And it's only at night
   One may venture away:
But think when the shadow
   Falls dark from the tree,
There is one near the meadow
   That's waiting for Thee:
But although you may love me
   It secret must be,
For no mortal must know
   You are waiting for me.

The villagers all
   Are so fond of their talk;
They'd jest for a month
   If they saw us two walk;

They 'd jest for a month
　　And a something would find,
If we even shook hands,
　　Or but look'd the least kind ;
So whate'er they may guess,
　　Or pretend they may see :
Still let nobody know
　　You are thinking of me.

WAIT TILL I PUT ON MY BONNET.

My father loves counting his cattle,
    My mother, she's fond of her chair,
But I, oh! I dote upon moonlight,
    Sweet walks, and the soft quiet air;
The field with the dew-star upon it,
    The scent of the newly-mown hay;
Oh, wait till I put on my bonnet,
    Night's sweeter by far than the day!
There are bonnets with ribbon and feather,
    But mine's like a gipsy's, so brown;
A bonnet that's careless of weather,
    But happy's the head 'neath its crown.

The day was intended for labour,
    But night was a gift to the heart;
When neighbour might visit with neighbour,
    And love have its whisper apart:

Then life finds a bloom still upon it,
    And time walks in silver array;
Oh, wait till I put on my bonnet,
    Night's sweeter by far than the day!
There are bonnets with ribbon and feather,
    But mine's like a gipsy's, so brown;
A bonnet that's careless of weather,
    But happy's the head 'neath its crown.

THE GARDEN STREAM.

A stream that pass'd a garden side—
   A wild young stream, for ever singing—
Where bloom'd a rose-tree in its pride,
   With crimson buds around it springing:
Oh! tell me why the streamlet flows,
   With notes so sweet I fear to lose 'em?
Is it because the blooming rose
   Is imaged on its tuneful bosom?

Yes; Beauty fills the world with song!
   The stream's young wave had flow'd in sadness;
For what is life, however long,
   Without the love which yields it gladness?
What charm can make the hours so blest?
   What wing so fair hath so much fleetness?
O Love! thine image in his breast,
   First fill'd the life of man with sweetness.

THE HAND OF A FRIEND.

Oh! Life's humble dwelling would seem indeed bare,
If the bright rose of Friendship entwined not its door:
And Misery's self would find residence there,
If Friendship's glad voice might inspire it no more!
Then, wherever the star of my destiny shine,—
Whether pleasures await me, or perils attend,—
Whilst one lingering pulse of existence is mine,
Oh, give me the hand and the heart of a Friend!

If sorrow sit dark on our spirit, what sound
Like the footstep of Friendship to chase it afar?
If danger surround us, still safety is found
In the light and the guidance of Friendship's true star.
Then, wherever the light of my destiny shine,—
Whether pleasures await me, or perils attend,—
Whilst one lingering pulse of existence is mine,
Oh, give me the hand and the heart of a Friend!

WIFE OF THE PIRATE.

'GAINST the rocky ribs of the rolling sea,
    The foundering vessel wore,
And many a heart in agony
    Grew cold and palsied o'er,
As rush'd the fate, which none might flee,
    Athwart that stormy shore!

Still many a distant beacon threw
    Its friendly light in vain,
And youthful eyes, to sorrow new,
    Gazed on in hopeless pain,
As wild the foamy billows flew
    Along that dreadful main!

Yet not more loving heart than thine,
    Joanna, sought that strand!
Thy beacon, like affection's shrine,
    Shed brightness o'er the land,
But none might light that stormy brine
    Save Heaven's almighty hand!

Slow fled the weary hours of night,
  As they would never go;
'Till pale upon the topmost height
  Morn show'd her face of woe,
As though she wept the bitter sight
  Of aching hearts below!

Still Oscar came not—still no sail
  The distant waves display;
But fast the morn grew calm and pale,
  The winds lull'd with the day,
'Till the last murmur of the gale
  Died slow and sad away!

At length a lorn and shatter'd barque
  The night breeze swept ashore;
'Twas marvel how, amidst the dark,
  Without or mast or oar,
It found the Pirate's rocky ark,
  Or saved the crew it bore!

Joanna rush'd—she gain'd the place
  Where they the storm-boat cast—
She rush'd to clasp in fond embrace
  Her loved—her lord—at last!
And wild she gazed upon each face,
  'Till every hope had past!

Oh, Oscar! Oscar! where was he?
  A prisoner!—and alone!
And they could leave him, thus to be
  In Wolfe's stern dungeon thrown!
She heard—a shriek was on the sea
  Far wilder than its own!

THE DAWN.

'Tis sweet when the twilight descends like a maiden,
   With star-sandall'd feet and cloud-mantle of gray;
When the skies seem with grandeur and mystery laden,
   But there's nothing so sweet as the dawn of the day.

Oh, if there's an hour to man's spirit appealing,
   An hour that can all his devotion repay,
'Tis when harmony, beauty, and grace are revealing
   Their charms at the dawn, the bright dawn of the day!

For it beam'd on the birth of Eve's fairest of daughters,
   It woke the first breath of the lark's matin-lay;
When the Spirit of God moved the face of the waters,
   All Eden lay blest in the dawn of the day.

Though the Noon, like a monarch enthroned, may assemble
    His sun-banner'd hosts in their gorgeous array;
Though the Moon may win hearts they are hearts that dissemble;
    For there's nothing so fair as the dawn of the day.

The dawn of the day, when the old man is waking,
    World-weary and languid, bereft of each stay;
When he turns to a dawn yet immortally breaking,
    The GOD-promised dawn of a heavenly day.

Oh, if harmony, beauty, and freshness are blending
    Their charms for the dawn of *our* care-compass'd way,
What bliss must be theirs who, through JESUS ascending,
    Behold with archangels the dawn of *His* day!

VOYAGE OF LIFE.

The golden sails of Thought,
    Fill'd with enchanted wind,
Swept to the land they sought—
    Each shore and realm of mind!
Youth sat the helm above,
    And mark'd each glorious trace—
All beauty—feeling—love—
    All poetry and grace!

The weary sails of Thought
    Were out upon the dark,
'Neath sky of storm inwrought,
    With, wild and wide, a spark :
A star that might prevail
    To point where dangers heaved.
'Twas Manhood reef'd the sail,
    And mourn'd for Youth deceived.

The shatter'd sails of Thought,
    All riven, went aground;
No shore that Youth had sought,
    No port that Manhood found,
Proved like that heaven which shone
    On golden sails of yore!
No; Life's romance was gone!
    Youth's poetry was o'er!

THE LONELY HOME.

There's none to say " good night" to me—
    No friend my little fire to share;
The old hoarse clock ticks drearily,
    And makes the silence worse to bear.
Gone! all are gone!—the fondest, best,
    And loveliest that I call'd mine own:
After brief suffering they're at rest;
    They—*they* lived not to wail alone!

Alone, alone—morn, noon, and eve
    I see the cold chairs keep their place;
I watch the dusty spider weave,
    Where once there shone a household grace.
The brightness of my home is dull—
    The busy faces all are gone;
I gaze—and oh! my heart is full—
    My aching heart, that breaks alone!

I ope the Bible, gray with age—
    The same my hapless grandsire read;
But tears stain fast and deep that page
    Which keeps *their* names—my loved—my dead!
The wandering stranger by my door—
    The passing tread—the distant tone—
All human sounds but deepen more
    The feeling I am lone—alone!

My cot with mantling ivy green,
    Its pleasant porch, its sanded floor—
Ah! Time's dread touch hath changed the scene,
    What *was*, alas! is now no more!
The key hath rusted in the lock,
    So long since I the threshold cross'd:
Why should I see the sun but mock
    The blessed light my home hath lost?

Oh! would my last low bed were made!
    But Death forsakes the lone and old;
Seeks the blithe cheek of youth to fade,
    To crush the gay, the strong, the bold.
Yet sometimes through the long dull night,
    When hours find supernatural tone,
I hear a promise of delight:
    Thou, GOD! Thou leav'st me not alone.

The wintry rain fell dull and deep,
    As slow a coffin pass'd the road;
No mourner there was seen to weep—
    No follower to that last abode!
Yet there a broken heart found peace—
    The peace that but in death it knew!
Alas! that human loves increase
    Our human woes and miseries too!

WHICH HOME?

Oh, none shall have a better home,
    Or brighter lot than thine!
None richer dress wherein to roam,
    Or jewels more divine!
Attendants gay shall lead the way,
    Where'er thy steps appear;
And life shall be a dream of May—
    And May last all the year!

A lofty home would suit me not;
    My heart would lonely be;
And pine to gain its humble cot—
    Its humble friends to see!
And oh, there's one—though far he's gone
    Across the severing wave;
For whose dear sake, I'd die ere break
    The parting vow I gave!

Should I, for gold, my faith withhold,
    And blight a heart so true,
What proof have ye I should not be
    As false, ere long, to you?
A gem more fair than queens can wear
    Is truth in woman's eye;
That gem so dear, so sweet, sincere,
    I'll keep until I die!

THE WORLDLY VOICE.

Ye early Dews of Morn,
Sweet wanderers from a bright and better sphere,
Why weep ye o'er the rude leaf, worn and sere—
   Ye that in heaven were born?

Oh, thou weak, spendthrift Rose,
Why waste thine odours on the careless night?
Exchanging perfume for unwholesome blight—
   Rubb'd by each wind that blows!

Sad Ivy, quit this spot!
Nor wander lorn by porch and abbey;
Why o'er the dead must thy fond shadow fall?
   The *Dead* can serve thee not!

"Peace, peace! thou Worldly Voice:
The Dews of Morn have their brief mission given;
Their part fulfill'd, they soar again to heaven,
   And bid new spheres rejoice."

"Be hush'd!" replied the Rose.
"Like deeds by generous hearts in secret done,
I glad the path of those the selfish shun,
　And lend what Heaven bestows!"

"Oh, Voice from love debarr'd!"
Rejoin'd the Ivy—"Voice the World respects—
I love to shield the Worth which Pride neglects,
　And serve without reward!

"Return, thou Voice, and prove
One simple truth to calculating Man—
Without reward, to do what good he can,
　Is GOD's first law of love!"

Heard where'er life hath trod—
Dew, Flower, and Leaf, that holy theme convey:
Oh, what were Man, if Man would but obey
　Thee, Nature—and his GOD!

NE'ER WILL I FORSAKE THEE, MOTHER.

Ne'er will I forsake thee, mother,
    Dear thy closing life shall be ;
Never will I love another
    As my heart now loveth thee !

Say'st thou that I speak but blindly ?
    For its truth I here engage :
Thou my youth hast nourish'd kindly,
    And I will console thine age !

Live we for our own good only ?
    Still receive yet nothing give ?
Shall I leave thee old and lonely ?
    Never, mother, whilst I live !

Still with thee I'll roam the wild wood,
    Still thy growing cares assuage ;
What thou wert unto my childhood,
    That I will be to thine age !

A LAMENT.

Go, number the clouds which the winds rend apart,
    Count the raindrops which fall o'er the desolate leaves;
They are light to the sorrows that visit the heart,
    They are few to the tears which no solace relieves.

Alas! for the man who devotedly twines
    Every chord of his heart round one object alóne ;
Yet must watch o'er her life as it hourly declines,
    That life which is dearer by far than his own!

Oh! teach me, great Nature, less feeling to keep;
    Strike the heart with some barrenness yet undescried :
For affection is sorrow,—to love is to weep,—
    Man never placed fondness on aught—but it died!

FIRST EMOTIONS.

If to be wishful still to linger near thee,
    And in thy absence every moment tell—
If when thou speak'st, it is new life to hear thee!
    If *this* be love—why, then, I love thee well.

If to gaze on when unaware thou seemeth;
    Toying with hawk or hound, by rock or fell;
Moving or lingering still like one that dreameth!
    If this be love—then do I love thee well!

To deem him blest, who, as his own might claim thee,
    And round thy path be privileged to dwell;
To be all tremor, if I hear one *name* thee!—
    If this be love—I *love*—and love thee well!

THE DOOMED CITY.

'Twas midnight on the waveless sea,
    Which bathed the citadel;
Over ocean and over land,
    The calm of slumber fell.

A light dawn'd in the scowling west:
    A red and flashing light,
Like a star—but it broader spread—
    It was no star of night.

A spirit came rushing through sea and cloud,
    On wings of might it flew:
And a glory over the soundless deep,
    Like a robe of lightning threw:

Broader and broader spread that flame,
    As it swept to the shore more near;
Earth and sky seem'd voiceless with awe,
    Before that thing of fear!

A ship! I beheld her skeleton sides,
  And her deck with beings rife;
Whose hearts through their fleshless ribs appear'd,
  Throbbing, and warm with life!

A ship! a ship! like a meteor she pass'd,
  With ruin upon her speed;
Her tatter'd sails, like dead men's shrouds,
  To the silent night were freed.

There was not a wave on the sea,
  There was not a breath of air,
Yet rapidly, rapidly sail'd that ship,
  As both wind and tide were there.

It seem'd as some horrible spell,
  On my fear-fraught vision lay;
Worlds I'd have given to quit that spot,
  Yet I could not turn away.

There was one man gain'd the shore—
  And the earth grew black and rank—
There was one wild rush of wind and wave,
  And the ship and her dread crew sank!

Then swiftly I fled the city,
  In deep and fearful pain;
And many dark months flew over my head,
  Ere I saw her proud towers again.

Meanwhile Death had despoil'd her halls,
  Through her wide streets grass had grown;
And of all her grace and majesty,
  Her strong towers remain'd alone.

I saw the dead lying in heaps,
  The aged, the young, and the fair;
I ask'd what that sight might mean,
  They told me the Plague had been there.

They told me the night and hour
  When the pestilence first spread:
I knew 'twas the night I had seen the ship;
  I knew 'twas the hour I had fled.

And a curse came over that city,
  The strength of her towers fell low;
And over the pride of her palaces,
  The dark waves of ocean flow.

LOVE UNTOLD.

My joy, yet grief! my rose, and yet my thorn!
   My soul's sweet day, and yet my spirit's night!
While thou stand'st by, I sigh as one forlorn—
   Yet when afar, I languish for thy sight.
Apart from thee, my heart can find no cheer,
Yet starts with tremour when thy step is near!

I dream of thee, yet *lose* thee in my dreams,
   And waking, ask of fate *if this must be?*
The realm of feeling hath unnumber'd streams,
   And every stream but bears my thought to thee:
Yet did thy form appear—my feet would stray,
As if they loved thee not, *another way!*

There is a constant fever in my breast,
   A something hoped, which dies when hope is given;
A sweet delight, and yet a strange unrest;
   A thought that trembles betwixt earth and heaven.
Would I loved less; or would the power were here
To own my love—and triumph over fear!

THE SNOW SHIP.

Far within the Northern main,
    Belted thick with ice and snow,
Fetter'd by a frozen chain,
    Many a fathom down below,
Fix'd 'mid hills and vales of Frost,
    See a stately ship appears!
Long amidst the glaciers lost—
    None may say how many years!
Wildly gleams that ship of snow,
Where the northern whirlwinds blow!

Set with stars the slippery sail,
    Strung with gems each rope and line:
Shimmering in the polar gale,
    Like some brilliant crystal mine.
Arch o'erhanging arch, between
    Stands a solid bridge of glass,
Midway earth and heaven seen,
    As for angel feet to pass

Down to save that ship of snow,
When the Arctic whirlwinds blow!

Many a breaking heart was there,
    Lock'd within that realm of death;
Many a long, imploring prayer
    Pass'd, with many a passing breath;
Never yet might mortal tell
    Whom that fated vessel bore;
Ocean keeps her secrets well,
    Deep and dark for evermore!
Whilst the mast, like spire of snow,
Points to heaven from human woe!

THUS NATURE SPEAKS.

Thus Nature speaks—thus, since the world began,
Her spirit led the aspiring thought of man !
Whether the Star of Science lit the way,
And oped the gates of an immortal day,
Or moved by Harmony's celestial hand,
The poet's song first triumph'd o'er the land,
It matters not—to Him be all the praise,
Who spread this heaven of stars to human gaze;
Lavish'd the wonders of Almighty thought
Over that world His word in glory wrought:
Who to the artist lent a spark divine,
And said—" Behold, this beauteous earth is thine ! "
To Him should poetry uplift its gaze,
To Him philosophy still utter praise ;
It matters not which first, which best, we find,
If Truth exalt and Wisdom rule the mind.
Let not contention jar man's fleeting hour,
But give the praise to Him who gave the power !

HYMN TO THE CROSS.

Of the world-redeeming Cross,
    Hear, ye nations of the free,
Where Atlantic billows toss,
    List, ye dwellers on the sea,
For the mission of our Saviour hath pass'd;
    And hath scatter'd o'er the plain
    Its false temples, rent in twain,
    With their idol gods profane,
        Like the blast!

In no chariot of cloud,
    With its whirlwind-wheels of flame,
Whilst the conscious mountains bow'd,
    He, the great Messiah, came!
But the meekest star of heaven shed its glow,
    And the leafless boughs did wave
    O'er the Mightiest to save,—
    O'er the Conqueror of the grave,—
        Sleeping low!

He spoke—and demons fled
   From the vengeance of His word;
And the wild graves of the dead
   Shrank and trembled as they heard,
For the mystery of GOD was on His breath:
   Although priest and scribe denied,
   In the madness of their pride,
   What the gates of hell knew wide,—
      And deep Death.

My SAVIOUR is my song,
   Who the mount of faith hath rear'd;
Who hath stricken down the strong,
   And the lost and lowly cheer'd;
Descending like a dove upon their souls!
   When the orphan's wail was sore;
   And the wreck'd and wind-beat shore
   Heard the cry of those no more,
      CHRIST consoles.

And they to whom the morn
   Brought no beauty—lent no light—
At His *touch* their world was born:
   For their JESUS gave them sight;

And the lame through the flow'ry meads could run;
And the deaf, who never heard
A fond mother's grateful word;
And the dumb—sang like the bird
To the sun!

Yet He, the Son of God—
That immortal blessings shed,
Whilst the wilderness He trod—
Knew not where to lay His head,
Though the wild lynx and leopard had their lair.
But the heavens bow'd, and came
At a whisper of His Name;
And sleep mantled His worn frame,
Even there!

The Eastern monarch lay
Amid gold and purple bound,
Whilst a myriad lamps, like day,
Shed a summer softness round;
And vassals throng'd in thousands at his tone.
But the mockery that lies
In rich gems and ophir dyes,
When Jehovah opes the skies,
Will be shown!

HYMN TO THE CROSS.

As was prophesied of old,
   So its coming soon may be,
When the arrogant and bold
   Shall grow weak o'er land and sea;
And the conquest-shout of empire be unknown;
   The devouring sword no more,
   Nor war's arrows, drunk with gore,
   Scatter carnage, as of yore,
      For a throne!

Wild shouts through Sion ran,
   Mid the zealot's scoff and gibe,
When the " cursed " of God and man,
   Sold his SAVIOUR for a bribe!
Where the fatal tree frown'd dark 'neath the sky,
   As, all bruised and bound, they led
   Their REDEEMER, blood to shed—
   The heavens veil'd their head
      Upon high!

And the mighty mountains fell
   With an earthquake-voice of woe;
And the buried rose to tell
   All the horror guilt must know;

But, lightning-writ, it spoke where'er they trod :
"Let the shuddering seas proclaim,
And the hills, struck dark with shame,
In their far depths own the name
Of their GOD!"

HERMIONE.

Majestic o'er the wild ravine,
    Where every object frowns sublime,
Dark Geierstein's massive towers are seen;
    Fierce relic of the feudal time!
There oft the Alpine vulture wings
    From gulf to gulf its fearful flight;
And surging down, the torrent flings
    Its waves a myriad feet in height!
Sever'd by earthquake long ago,
    The rocks like giants stretch below;
Some, sharper than the keenest brand,
    Jagg'd and torn, and splinter'd lie;
Some lift their tall points to the sky—
    Like Nature's spires—that awe the land!

Full many a dark and sinful tale
    Of murder done at midnight hour,
Of traveller wilder'd in the gale
    That beats around that stormy tower;

Things that the listener's cheek will blanch !
And whilst the thundering avalanche
   Shakes Nature, as with terror's throes
They tell him—e'en his trembling breath
May loose the shaft that threatens death
   Within the Alpine snows !
'Twas once beneath that massive pile—
   When gallant knight and lady fair
   Had met the bridal feast to share,
And cheer the hours with song and smile—
   That strange events, they say, occurr'd,
   More wild than ever mortal heard !

The Baron of that grim domain
   Had sought and won a matchless bride—
One any heart had joy'd to gain !
   One worthy all her husband's pride !
Upon her soft ingenuous cheek
Were writ, more clear than tongue may speak,
Feelings that could not brook control;
Those warm emotions of the soul
That leave sweet tears within the eyes !
A heart that thinks not of disguise,
But loves, and pours its happy light
On all things ; making life more bright !
   Earth nearer to the skies !

Surely a nature thus endow'd,
So far beyond the meaner crowd,
Might 'scape the poison Envy throws;
For how could breast like hers find foes?
Alas! there's many a thing on earth
We never could believe had birth,
But that Experience hourly tells
Of deeds 'gainst which Belief rebels!
And malice, envy, spleen, and strife,
Tread still the tragic stage of life!

Something was said of " angel form,"
Of vernal beauty, fond and warm,
· Of footsteps born for angel path—
When Steinfeldt's Countess rose in wrath:—
" Speak not to me of angel worth—
I tell ye she's of Demon birth!
   The Baron hath his rank demean'd!
Away, and shun the enchanter's breath,
For in it lurks eternal death!
Destruction launches from her gaze,
Those eyes emit unholy rays!
That *opal* round her dazzling neck
Was wrought by Demon hands, to deck
   The bosom of a fiend!

"Go, take her, where the Just have trod,
Before the altar of our GOD;
Go! cross and sign the Sorceress now
With sacred water on the brow;
Then brace these limbs upon the rack
If One spring not to claim her back,
 Whose power *she* recks full well!
Whose throne in curses was conceived,
Whose rule Eternal Sin achieved,
 With Demon hosts of hell!

" The Daughter of Dännischemend,
 Say, had she not a Magian sire
Sworn by the pangs that never end,
 By altar of consuming fire,
The laws of Lucifer to hold—
A sire that sold his soul for gold?

" Haste! to the altar with this bride,
 Who ne'er will rest in Christian tomb!"
And ere a living lip replied,
 The lady vanish'd from the room!

In ire the Baron straight uprose,
 And frown'd as if on mortal foes;

Scarce one, he thought, of all his guests,
Would prove a friend ! *though friend profest!*
Unsheathing stern his trenchant blade,
Lowering on all the lamps display'd—
" Ho ! lives there knight or peer," he cried,
" Who dare repeat—or will defend
These impious falsehoods 'gainst my bride?
If one—then never Truth had friend !
For, oh ! if e'er on human head
The boundless grace of heaven was shed ;
If ever heart from stain were free,
'Tis thine, my wrong'd Hermione ! "

The Baron gazed from side to side,
But not one lip of all replied.
 " Then since no living hand is found
To aid that lie's malicious power,
E'en let it perish with the hour—
 Too weak a foe to keep its ground !
But yet, if further proof we need
To strangle Hate which *might* succeed.
Go, call your mistress—say we wait
Her presence at the Chapel-gate—
There to receive the holy rite,
With others of our guests to-night !

"A sorceress? oh, detested tongue!
  A fiend? just Heaven, and can it be,
That all this infamy and wrong,
  Is pour'd on one so pure as thee,
  My own, my loved Hermione!"

She came! O Beauty, whence is given
  That speaking loveliness of frame?
  That grace—that charm—without a name?
That purity which breathes of heaven?
  She came! the Baron marks her cheek;
And up the chapel aisle he wends;
  In strange suspense—too wild to speak—
Fast follow'd by his wondering friends!
Now by the holy fount he stands—
Now lifts the water in his hands,
And o'er each beauteous feature throws
Its drops like dews upon the rose!
In faith and trusting kindness thrown;
But, oh! *that shriek*—it pierced the stone!
The marble walls, as with one tongue,
Echoed that horrid wail along!
The woods, the rocks, the gulfs around,
A moment more prolonged that sound;
Then sank it from the curdling air,
In silence deep as earth's despair!

Those *Gems* that flash'd with magic fire,
In agony of light expire!
As though a *human pang* was sent
Throughout their burning element!
And she—the beautiful and bright—
　Lay by that holy fountain head,
Like dust upon the howling night!
　Like ashes on which fiends have fed!
And horror seized the Baron's mind,
　A weight oppress'd his sinking brain;
He stagger'd forth like one struck blind—
A wreck!—an outcast from mankind!
And none might follow on his track,
And none dared warn, or urge him back!
Nor of his fate record but this,
That half way down the sheer abyss,
The Alpine vulture gorged full deep,
Holding a hideous banquet there,
While fiends laugh'd loud in upper air!
And oft, lone startled from their sleep,
Men hear at midnight hour, 'tis said,
The long-lost Baron's spectral tread;
And watch his bleeding footsteps glide,
Still seeking for his Phantom Bride!

GOD HELP THE ORPHAN.

God help the orphan,
  Homeless and desolate,
  Few to commiserate,
God help the orphan!
  Sad to be brotherless,
  Woe to be motherless;
God help the orphan!

Thou, in whom love doth dwell,
Deeper than tongue can tell;
  Help Thou the orphan!
Fatherless none can be,
Whilst in eternity
Ruleth the Deity,
  None can be fatherless!
Dews of Thy mercy shed
On the poor orphan's head;

GOD HELP THE ORPHAN.

Bid him still kneel to Thee,
Look up to heaven, and see,
Though those he loved are gone,
Still there is ever ONE
    Feels for the fatherless!

Blest be the PRAYER Thou 'st given,
" FATHER, who art in heaven ; "
Oh, in our utmost need,
Father art Thou indeed ;
Ever when lonely thus,
Sending some friend to us ;
Soothing, consoling us ;
Thou, who art still the same,
Thou, whom our prayers doth claim,
" Hallowed be Thy Name,"
    GOD of the fatherless!

Thou, whom all hearts doth hold,
Touching with love the cold,
Prompting sweet pity's tear,
Ever in spirit near,
Guarding each tender frame,—
Bless'd be Thy holy Name,
    GOD of the fatherless!

Still through all life may we
Gratefully cling to Thee!
Thou, who from Heaven thus
Kindly hast given us
Friends, that like parents feel,
Watching the orphan's weal;
Friends, who commiserate,
Feel for the desolate:
Friends Thine own hand hath given,
" Father, who art in heaven;"
Ever Thy Name we bless,
God of the Fatherless,
Guide of the Motherless,
   Help of the Orphan!

LINES ON THE DEATH

OF

HENRY DRINKWATER BIRCH,

AGED SEVEN YEARS.

Oh! the lost—they leave life drear,
    Evermore—evermore :
    Nothing can restore
That which made existence dear :
Pass'd—like music on the ear—
    Evermore !
With the angels evermore,
    Evermore !

Darkness hath the soul o'erspread,
    Ever dark—ever dark ;
    Lost Hope's latest spark :
For the beautiful hath fled—
And a shadow wraps the dead—
    Ever dark !
But God's Word, to mourners said,
    Lights the dark !

FINIS.

Life's not our own—'tis but a loan—
    To be repaid!
Soon the dark Comer's at the door,
The debt is due—the dream is o'er—
    Life's but a shade!

Thus all decline—that bloom or shine—
    Both star and flower;
'Tis but a little odour shed—
A light gone out—a spirit fled—
    A funeral hour!

Then let us show a tranquil brow,
    Whate'er befalls:
That we upon Life's latest brink
May look on Death's dark face, and think
    An Angel calls!

James S. Virtue, Printer, City Road, London.

Now ready, Vol. I., demy 8vo., cloth, price 18s.,

HISTORY OF ENGLAND

DURING

THE REIGN OF GEORGE THE THIRD.

By JOHN GEORGE PHILLIMORE, Q.C.

OPINIONS OF THE PRESS.

"This volume gives promise of a work which will deserve to be read. In intention the book is good, in execution very good; unpleasant, perhaps, to the bigots of all parties, but acceptable to every man who may be glad to know what an honest thinker and a rough but able writer has to say about the time of George the Third."—*Athenæum*.

"Well worth reading, from the evident diligence with which it has been prepared, and the vigorous style which he has adopted."—*Critic*.

"Full of instructive material, which Mr. Phillimore handles with evident honesty of purpose, and sometimes with considerable power."—*Reader*.

"The number of references which he gives to the authorities he has consulted, furnishes conclusive proof that he has spared no pains to obtain the fullest and most authentic information which was most accessible to him. No one can read the present volume without hoping he may soon have its successor in his hands."—*Morning Advertiser*.

"In style, as in other respects, Mr. Phillimore is original. He writes with a vigour and freshness which carry you on. Altogether it is a clever, lively, and interesting book."—*Saturday Review*.

"The style is vigorous and spirited."—*Spectator*.

"We are bound to testify to the ability he displays. He is no careless writer; no hasty vamper up of second-hand facts and borrowed opinions. A book vigorously and ably written, which will be read with interest."—*Notes and Queries*.

"We are able to admire much of Mr. Phillimore's book. The subject that Mr. Phillimore really undertakes to discuss is handled with so much power, and is illustrated from so much careful reading, that his 'History,' when completed, will be thankfully accepted by all students of the period."—*Examiner*.

VIRTUE BROTHERS & CO., 1. AMEN CORNER.

Fcap. 8vo., 7s. 6d., cloth lettered,

NAOMI; or, the Last Days of Jerusalem.

By MRS. J. B. WEBB.

New Edition, with Designs by GILBERT, and View and Plan of Jerusalem.

"It is in truth an admirable little volume, and well worthy of a yet more extensive patronage than it has already received."—*Maidstone Journal.*

"One of the most interesting works we have read for some time. We are not surprised at the popularity it has attained; it deserves it, and we cordially wish it further success."—*Metropolitan.*

"The plot is easy, natural, and well sustained. The narrative gracefully written. . . . Seldom have we read a tale better adapted for its purpose."—*Monthly Review.*

In super-royal 8vo., price 10s. 6d., cloth gilt; or 21s. in morocco,

WALKS ABOUT JERUSALEM AND ITS ENVIRONS

Illustrated by Twenty-four Engravings on Steel, Two Maps, and many superior Woodcuts.

"We have at length in this attractive volume the *desideratum* of a complete picturesque guide to the topography of Jerusalem."—*Patriot.*

"The volume is well got up in point of embellishments, and contains much valuable matter, with illustrations beautifully executed."—*Church of England Magazine.*

"Our impression is, that Jerusalem was never before so successfully delineated."—*Evangelical Magazine.*

In fcap. 8vo., price 5s., cloth gilt,

THE PRINCE OF THE HOUSE OF DAVID;

OR, THREE YEARS IN THE HOLY CITY.

Edited by the Rev. Professor J. H. INGRAHAM, Rector of St. John's Church, Mobile. Illustrated with Engravings.

"Our perusal of it has been only to impress us with the ability of the author in the use of the materials, and in the structure of a pleasing and most affecting tale."—*Clerical Journal.*

"This is the best production of its class that has come to our hands for a long time, and it is but candid and just to say that it adds very much to the stores of knowledge already existing about the East."—*British Standard.*

"We hardly know what to say about this book; it is written in beautiful style, and it conveys much valuable information as to the customs and manners of the inhabitants of the Holy Land."—*Wesleyan Times.*

"The whole is written in a semi-poetical style, which will prove attractive to religious readers."—*Leader.*

"The volume contains much information as to Jewish manners and customs."—*Baptist Magazine.*

"Professor Ingraham has worked out his plan with diligence and reverence."—*Literary Gazette.*

VIRTUE BROTHERS & CO., 1, AMEN CORNER.

Just ready, fcap. 8vo., antique cloth, price 3s. 6d.,

PATTIE DURANT: a Tale of 1662.

By "CYCLA."

Author of "Aunt Dorothy's Will," "Passing Clouds," "Warfare and Work."

"A very neatly told story in the antique style, illustrative of the state of the religious belief among the people of England during the periods immediately preceding and following the Act of Uniformity."—*Daily News.*

"One of the charms of this handsomely got-up little volume is the simplicity of style in which it is written. We question much if larger works on the Act of Uniformity will be read with greater pleasure and profit than the excellent and artless contents of Pattie Durant's diary. As a drawing-room table book, the tale of Pattie Durant is eminently worthy of commendation."—*Morning Advertiser.*

"Pattie, the heroine, is throughout charmingly drawn; cheerful, loving, devoting herself to the good of others, Pattie's piety is such as we could wish for all the daughters of our English homes. It is more than a healthy book—it is a truly worthy and valuable book, and we hope it will find its way to many parlours and drawing-rooms."—*Patriot.*

"We have had more than once, in these columns, to commend to our readers the productions of 'Cycla.' We are glad to say, however, that, both for the interest of the story and for the skill and simplicity with which it is unfolded, Pattie Durant far excels any of its predecessors."—*Freeman.*

In 1 Vol., crown 8vo. cloth, 7s. 6d.,

TWICE LOST: a Novel.

By S. M., Author of "Use of Sunshine," "Story of a Family," "Queen Isabel," &c.

"Another first-rate novel by a woman! The plot well-conceived and worked out, the characters individualised and clear-cut, and the story so admirably told that you are hurried along for two hours and a half with a smile often breaking out at the humour, a tear ready to start at the pathos, and with unflagging interest, till the heroine's release from all trouble is announced at the end. . . . We heartily recommend the book to all readers. It is more full of character than any book we remember since Charles Reade's Christie Johnstone."—*Reader.*

"The personages have all of them a certain look of reality, and there is a notion of likeness which ensures the reader's interest."—*Athenæum.*

"The plot of this tale is an original one, and well worked out. . . . We can sincerely recommend this tale; it is quite out of the general run of books, and is sure to prove an interesting one."—*Observer.*

"This is a striking story. It has a freshness and originality about it, which are very pleasant."—*Morning Advertiser.*

"Without being a sensation novel, this is a most exciting and attractive story."—*Daily News.*

VIRTUE BROTHERS & CO., 1, AMEN CORNER.

New and Improved Edition, with Frontispiece, 18mo., price 1s. 6d. cloth gilt,

NURSERY RHYMES.

An ILLUSTRATED EDITION, in large type, with Sixteen Cuts by GILBERT, 16mo., price 2s. 6d. cloth, gilt edges.

By the same Authors,

ORIGINAL POEMS FOR INFANT MINDS.

New and Improved Edition, with Frontispiece, Two Vols., 18mo., price 1s. 6d. each, cloth gilt.

Fourteenth Edition, corrected and enlarged, 18mo., price 2s. 6d. cloth; or 3s. scarlet, gilt edges,

SELECT POETRY FOR CHILDREN.

With brief Explanatory Notes, arranged for the use of Schools and Families.

By JOSEPH PAYNE.

New and Enlarged Edition, fcap. 8vo., price 5s. cloth, red edges,

STUDIES IN ENGLISH POETRY;

With short Biographical Sketches, and Notes Explanatory and Critical, intended as a Text-book for the higher Classes in Schools, and as an Introduction to the Study of English Literature.

By JOSEPH PAYNE.

"The work is deserving of commendation, as comprehending much that is excellent—the very flowers and gems of English poetry—and nothing exceptionable."

"The plan and the execution are equally good; altogether it is an excellent reading book of poetry."—*Watchman.*

VIRTUE BROTHERS & CO., 1, AMEN CORNER.

www.ingramcontent.com/pod-product-compliance
Lightning Source LLC
Chambersburg PA
CBHW020227240426
43672CB00006B/438